Praise for Neil Jordan

The Crying Game

"Amazing. Neil Jordan's romantic thriller is a brilliant original
. . . dazzling . . . a complex, challenging love story."
　　　　　　　—Janet Maslin, *The New York Times*

"Mind-popping . . . masterfully constructed. Nothing compares to
the tonal tightrope walk of *The Crying Game,* which seems to
contain four movies for the price of one, each full of surprises."
　　　　　　　—David Ansen, *Newsweek*

"Jordan's script is a marvel of glancing nuance and telling echo
. . . A Shakespearian movie of miraculous transformations, divest-
ments, guns, haircuts, love. It is a career achievement for Jordan."
　　　　　　　—David Lyons, *Film Comment*

"Neil Jordan is one of a kind. At heart, he is a madly unrecon-
structed romantic in [whose] view the power of love can work
miracles. Jordan's screenplay is both efficient and ingenious."
　　　　　　　—Vincent Canby, *The New York Times*

"Neil Jordan is one of the great romantics of contemporary
cinema."
　　　　　　　　　　　　　　　　　　　—*Elle*

"A tale unique in virtually every respect . . . An astonishing, dizzy-
ingly romantic thriller . . . fresh and endlessly fascinating."
　　　　　　　　　　　　　　　—*Cosmopolitan*

"An exceptional film that is by turns darkly funny and deeply
affecting."　　　　　　　　—Peter Travers, *Rolling Stone*

About the Author

NEIL JORDAN was born in Sligo, Ireland, in 1950. He has published two novels, *The Past* and *The Dream of a Beast*; his collection of short stories, *Night in Tunisia*, won the Guardian Fiction prize in 1979. Jordan's first film, *Angel*, was described by *The London Times* as "one of the most accomplished debuts from an English-language film-maker this side of the Atlantic in the past decade." Jordan's other films include *The Company of Wolves, Mona Lisa, High Spirits, We're No Angels, The Miracle*, and the Oscar-nominated *The Crying Game*. Jordan is currently working on a new novel and preparing the film version of Anne Rice's *Interview with the Vampire*.

INTERNATIONAL

A Neil Jordan Reader

Night in Tunisia and Other Stories

The Dream of a Beast

The Crying Game

VINTAGE INTERNATIONAL
Vintage Books
A Division of Random House, Inc.
New York

Library of Congress Cataloging-in-Publication Data
Jordan, Neil, 1950–
    A Neil Jordan Reader / by Neil Jordan. — 1st
Vintage International ed.
        p.   cm.
    ISBN 0-679-74834-2
    I. Title.
PR6060.06255C78   1993
823'.914—dc20   93-2994
                        CIP

Contents

A Neil Jordan Reader

I TEND TO write scripts as sparely as possible, for two reasons. Firstly, the barer the language is the easier it is to concentrate on the essentials when directing what you've written. And those essentials I would define as what is seen, what happens, and what is said. Secondly, because elaborate visual, psychological, or visceral description tends to confuse those you have to work with—designers, cinematographers, and, most importantly, actors. The kind of sentence that may be appropriate in a novel or a short story would be not only inappropriate, it would be misleading. To take an example from Kafka: "One day, Gregor Samsa woke to find himself transformed into an enormous beetle." One of the most beautiful and succinct sentences ever written, but one belonging to a world of realities that is most unhelpful to the filmmaker. The number of questions it raises are legion. It implies, for a start, a multitude of prior days on which Gregor Samsa woke up to find himself a human being. And assuming one could construct the beetle that does justice to Kafka's imagination, how does one convey that this beetle once was Gregor Samsa? How on earth does a beetle wake up?

This is not to say that these problems are insurmountable, merely that the linguistic realities with which Kafka deals are light-years away from those the scriptwriter must handle. Which again, I would define as what is seen, what happens, and what is said. There are, however, linguistic pleasures to be gleaned from scriptwriting—apart from those one reads about in screenwriting manuals about dramatic structure, the "arc" of the character (whatever that is), the first, second, and third act (why only three?), and so on. And those pleasures are to do with the application of language towards a quite specific purpose. When you strip it bare of all psychological implications and metaphoric weight, as you must, you are left with the heart of the matter: the accurate, succinct, and uncluttered description of what you wish to see on the screen. And for one who also writes prose, as I do, this can be as bracing as a cold shower on a December day.

Apart from language, of course, there is the story. And one could argue that the problems of narrative are the same for all fictions, written, spoken, or filmed. *The Crying Game* had a long gestation. I initially thought of the story after my first film, *Angel*, a story that arose out of the Northern Irish conflict, about a British soldier held hostage by an IRA activist. The situation had been dealt with twice before in Irish literature, by Frank O'Connor in a short story called "Guest Of The Nation" and by Brendan Behan in a play called *The Hostage*. The attraction of such a theme for Irish writers, the friendship that develops between two protagonists in a conflict, that grows paradoxically deeper than any of their other allegiances, lies in the broader history of Anglo-Irish relationships: two cultures in need of each other, yet at war with each other. The fact that such a theme can be as relevant in the twenties, for O'Connor, and in the fifties, for Behan, as in the nineties, for me, says more than I want to ponder about the current state of things. O'Connor and Behan dealt with simple friendship between two men. Underlying this friendship lay an erotic possibility, a sense of mutual need and identification that could have provided salvation for their protagonists. That possibility remained subdued, and so both stories ended tragically. With *The Crying Game*, I brought the erotic thread to the surface. Instead of two, there were now three. A hostage, a captor, and an absent lover. The lover became the focus for the erotic subtext, loved by both men in a way they couldn't love each other. And the story ended with a kind of happiness. I say a kind of happiness, because it involved the separation of a prison cell and other more profound separations, of racial, national, and sexual identity. But for the lovers, it was the irony of what divided them that allowed them to smile. So perhaps there is hope for our divisions yet.

Neil Jordan

Night

in

Tunisia

and Other Stories

To Vivienne Shields

Last Rites

ONE WHITE-HOT Friday in June at some minutes after five o'clock a young builder's labourer crossed an iron railway overpass, just off the Harrow Road. The day was faded now and the sky was a curtain of haze, but the city still lay hard-edged and agonisingly bright in the day's undiminished heat. The labourer as he crossed the overpass took note of its regulation shade of green. He saw an old, old negro immigrant standing motionless in the shade of a red-bricked wall. Opposite the wall, in line with the overpass, he saw the Victorian facade of Kensal Rise Baths. Perhaps because of the heat, or because of a combination of the heat and his temperament, these impressions came to him with an unusual clarity; as if he had seen them in a film or in a dream and not in real, waking life. Within the hour he would take his own life. And dying, a cut-throat razor in his hand, his blood mingling with the shower-water into the colour of weak wine he would take with him to whatever vacuum lay beyond, three memories: the memory of a green-painted bridge; of an old, bowed, shadowed negro; of the sheer tiled wall of a cubicle in what had originally been the wash-houses of Kensal Rise Tontine and Workingmen's Association, in what was now Kensal Rise Baths.

The extraordinary sense of nervous anticipation the labourer experienced had long been familiar with him. And, inexplicable. He never questioned it fully. He knew he anticipated something, approaching the baths. He knew that it wasn't quite pleasure. It was something more and less than pleasurable, a feeling of ravishing, private vindication, of exposure, of secret, solipsistic victory. Over what he never asked. But he knew. He knew as he approached the baths to wash off the dust of a week's labour, that this hour would be the week's high-point. Although during the week he never thought of it, never dwelt on its pleasures—as he did, for instance on his prolonged Saturday morning's rest—when the hour came it was as if the secret thread behind his week's existence was emerging into daylight, was exposing itself to the scrutiny of daylight, his daylight. The way the fauna of the sea-bed are exposed, when the tide goes out.

And so when he crossed the marble step at the door, when he faced the lady behind the glass counter, handing her sevenpence, accepting a ticket from her, waving his hand to refuse towel and soap, gesticulating towards the towel in his duffle-bag, each action was performed with the solemnity of an elaborate ritual, each action was a ring in the circular maze that led to the hidden purpose—the purpose he never elaborated, only felt; in his arm as he waved his hand; in his foot as he crossed the threshold. And when he walked down the corridor, with its white walls, its strange hybrid air, half unemployment exchange, half hospital ward, he was silent. As he took his place on the long oak bench, last in a line of negro, Scottish and Irish navvies his expression preserved the same immobility as theirs, his duffle-bag was kept between his feet and his rough slender hands between his knees and his eyes upon the grey cream wall in front of him. He listened to the rich, public voices of the negroes, knowing the warm colours of even their work-clothes without having to look. He listened to the odd mixture of reticence and resentment in the Irish voices. He felt the tiles beneath his feet, saw the flaking wall before him, the hard oak bench beneath him, the grey-haired cockney caretaker emerging every now and then from the shower-hall to call "Shower!," "Bath!" and at each call the next man in the queue rising, towel and soap under one arm. So plain, so commonplace, and underneath the secret pulsing—but his face was immobile.

As each man left the queue he shifted one space forward and each time the short, crisp call issued from the cockney he turned his head to stare. And when his turn eventually came to be first in the queue and the cockney called "Shower!" he padded quietly through the open door. He had a slow walk that seemed a little stiff, perhaps because of the unnatural straightness of his back. He had a thin face, unremarkable but for a kind of distance in the expression; removed, glazed blue eyes; the kind of inwardness there, of immersion, that is sometimes termed stupidity.

The grey-haired cockney took his ticket from him. He nodded towards an open cubicle. The man walked slowly through the rows of white doors, under the tiled roof to the cubicle signified. It was the seventh door down.

"Espera me, Quievo!"

"Ora, deprisa, ha?"

He heard splashing water, hissing shower-jets, the smack of palms off wet thighs. Behind each door he knew was a naked man, held timeless and separate under an umbrella of darting water. The fact of the walls, of the similar but totally separate beings behind those walls never ceased to amaze him; quietly to excite him. And the shouts of those who communicated echoed strangely through the long, perfectly regular hall. And he knew that everything would be heightened thus now, raised into the aura of the green light.

He walked through the cubicle door and slid the hatch into place behind him. He took in his surroundings with a slow familiar glance. He knew it all, but he wanted to be a stranger to it, to see it again for the first time, always the first time: the wall, evenly gridded with white tiles, rising to a height of seven feet; the small gap between it and the ceiling; the steam coming through the gap from the cubicle next door; the jutting wall, with the full-length mirror affixed to it; behind it, enclosed by the plastic curtain, the shower. He went straight to the mirror and stood motionless before it. And the first throes of his removal began to come upon him. He looked at himself the way one would examine a flat-handled trowel, gauging its usefulness;

or, idly, the way one would examine the cracks on a city pavement. He watched the way his nostrils, caked with cement-dust,
dilated with his breathing. He watched the rise of his chest, the
buttons of his soiled white work-shirt straining with each rise,
each breath. He clenched his teeth and his fingers. Then he
undressed, slowly and deliberately, always remaining in full
view of the full-length mirror.

After he was unclothed his frail body with its thin ribs, hard
biceps and angular shoulders seemed to speak to him, through
its frail passive image in the mirror. He listened and watched.

*Later it would speak, lying on the floor with open wrists, still
retaining its goose-pimples, to the old cockney shower-attendant
and the gathered bathers, every memory behind the transfixed
eyes quietly intimated, almost revealed, by the body itself. If they
had looked hard enough, had eyes keen enough, they would
have known that the skin wouldn't have been so white but for
a Dublin childhood, bread and margarine, cramped, carbonated
air. The feet with the miniature half-moon scar on the right
instep would have told, eloquently, of a summer spent on Laytown Strand, of barefoot walks on a hot beach, of sharded glass
and poppies of blood on the summer sand. And the bulge of
muscle round the right shoulder would have testified to two
years hod-carrying, just as the light, nervous lines across the
forehead proclaimed the lessons of an acquisitive metropolis, the
glazed eyes themselves demonstrating the failure, the lessons not
learnt. All the ill-assorted group of bathers did was pull their
towels more rigidly about them, noting the body's glaring pubes,
imagining the hair (blonde, maybe) and the skin of the girls that
first brought them to life; the first kiss and the indolent smudges
of lipstick and all the subsequent kisses, never quite recovering
the texture of the first. They saw the body and didn't hear the
finer details—just heard that it had been born, had grown and
suffered much pain and a little joy; that its dissatisfaction had
been deep; and they thought of the green bridge and the red-
bricked walls and understood—.*

He savoured his isolation for several full minutes. He allowed the cold to seep fully through him, after the heat of clothes, sunlight. He saw pale, rising goose-pimples on the mirrored flesh before him. When he was young he had been in the habit of leaving his house and walking down to a busy sea-front road and clambering down from the road to the mud-flats below. The tide would never quite reach the wall and there would be stretches of mud and stone and the long sweep of the cement wall with the five-foot-high groove running through it where he could sit, and he would look at the stone, the flat mud and the dried cakes of sea-lettuce and see the tide creep over them and wonder at their impassivity, their imperviousness to feeling; their deadness. It seemed to him the ultimate blessing and he would sit so long that when he came to rise his legs, and some-times his whole body, would be numb. He stood now till his immobility, his cold, became near-agonising. Then he walked slowly to the shower, pulled aside the plastic curtain and walked inside. The tiles had that dead wetness that he had once noticed in the beach-pebbles. He placed each foot squarely on them and saw a thin cake of soap lying in a puddle of grey water. Both were evidence of the bather here before him and he wondered vaguely what he was like; whether he had a quick, rushed shower or a slow, careful one; whether he in turn had wondered about the bather before him. And he stopped wondering, as idly as he had begun. And he turned on the water.

It came hot. He almost cried with the shock of it; a cry of pale, surprised delight. It was a pet love with him, the sudden heat and the wall of water, drumming on his crown, sealing him magi-cally from the world outside; from the universe outside; the pleasurable biting needles of heat; the ripples of water down his hairless arms; the stalactites gathering at each fingertip; wet hair, the sounds of caught breath and thumping water. He loved the pain, the total self-absorption of it and never wondered why he loved it; as with the rest of the weekly ritual—the trudge through the muted officialdom of the bath corridors into the solitude of the shower cubicle, the total ultimate solitude of the boxed, sealed figure, three feet between it and its fellow; the contradictory joy of the first impact of heat, of the pleasurable pain.

An overseer in an asbestos works who had entered his cubicle black and who had emerged with a white, blotchy, greyish skin-hue divined the reason for the cut wrists. He looked at the tiny coagulation of wrinkles round each eye and knew that here was a surfeit of boredom; not a moody, arbitrary, adolescent boredom, but that boredom which is a condition of life itself. He saw the way the mouth was tight and wistful and somehow uncommunicative, even in death, and the odour of his first contact with that boredom came back to him. He smelt again the incongruous fish-and-chip smells, the smells of the discarded sweet-wrappings, the metallic odour of the fun-palace, the sul-phurous whiff of the dodgem wheels; the empty, musing, poi-gnant smell of the seaside holiday town, for it was here that he had first met his boredom; here that he had wandered the green carpet of the golf-links, with the stretch of grey sky overhead, asking, what to do with the long days and hours, turning then towards the burrows and the long grasses and the strand, decid-ing there's nothing to do, no point in doing, the sea glimmering to the right of him like the dull metal plate the dodgem wheels ran on. Here he had lain in a sand-bunker for hours, his head making a slight indentation in the sand, gazing at the mordant procession of clouds above. Here he had first asked, what's the point, there's only point if it's fun, it's pleasure, if there's more pleasure than pain; then thinking of the pleasure, weighing up the pleasure in his adolescent scales, the pleasure of the greased fish-and-chip bag warming the fingers, of the sweet taken from the wrapper, the discarded wrapper and the fading sweetness, of the white flash of a pubescent girl's legs, the thoughts of touch and caress, the pain of the impossibility of both and his head digging deeper in the sand he had seen the scales tip in favour of pain. Ever so slightly maybe, but if it wins then what's the point. And he had known the sheep-white clouds scudding through the blueness and ever after thought of them as signifi-cant of the preponderance of pain; and he looked now at the white scar on the young man's instep and thought of the white clouds and thought of the bobbing girls' skirts and of the fact of pain—.

The first impact had passed; his body temperature had risen and the hot biting needles were now a running, massaging hand. And a silence had descended on him too, after the self-immersed orgy of the driving water. He knew this shower was all things to him, a world to him. Only here could he see this world, hold it in balance, so he listened to what was now the quietness of rain in the cubicle, the hushed, quiet sound of dripping rain and the green rising mist through which things are seen in their true, unnatural clarity. He saw the wet, flapping shower-curtain. There was a bleak rose-pattern on it, the roses faded by years of condensation into green: green roses. He saw the black spaces between the tiles, the plug-hole with its fading, whorling rivulet of water. He saw the exterior dirt washed off himself, the caked cement-dust, the flecks of mud. He saw creases of black round his elbow-joints, a high-water mark round his neck, the more permanent, ingrained dirt. And he listened to the falling water, looked at the green roses and wondered what it would be like to see those things, hear them, doing nothing but see and hear them; nothing but the pure sound, the sheer colour reaching him; to be as passive as the mud pebble was to that tide. He took the cake of soap then from the grilled tray affixed to the wall and began to rub himself hard. Soon he would be totally, bleakly clean.

There was a dash of paint on his cheek. The negro painter he worked beside had slapped him playfully with his brush. It was disappearing now, under pressure from the soap. And with it went the world, that world, the world he inhabited, the world that left grit under the nails, dust under the eyelids. He scrubbed at the dirt of that world, at the coat of that world, the self that lived in that world, in the silence of the falling water. Soon he would be totally, bleakly clean.

The old cockney took another ticket from another bather he thought he recognised. Must have seen him last week. He crumpled the ticket in his hand, went inside his glass-fronted office and impaled it onto a six-inch nail jammed through a block of wood. He flipped a cigarette from its packet and lit it, wheezing heavily. Long hours spent in the office here, the windows running with condensation, had exaggerated a bronchial condition. He let his eyes scan the seventeen cubicles. He wondered again how many of them, coming every week for seventeen weeks, have visited each of the seventeen showers. None, most likely. Have to go where they're told, don't they. No way they can get into a different box other than the one that's empty, even if they should want to. But what are the chances, a man washing himself ten years here, that he'd do the full round? And the chances that he'd be stuck to the one? He wrinkled his eyes and coughed and rubbed the mist from the window to see more clearly.

White, now. Not the sheet white of the tiles, but a human, flaccid, pink skin-white. He stood upwards, let his arms dangle by his sides, his wrists limp. His short black hair was plastered to his crown like a tight skull-cap. He gazed at the walls of his own cubicle and wondered at the fact that there were sixteen other cubicles around him, identical to this one, which he couldn't see. A man in each, washed by the same water, all in various stages of cleanliness. And he wondered did the form in the next cubicle think of him, his neighbour, as he did. Did he reciprocate his wondering. He thought it somehow appropriate that there should be men naked, washing themselves in adjacent cubicles, each a foreign country to the other. Appropriate to what, he couldn't have said. He looked round his cubicle and wondered: what's it worth, what does it mean, this cubicle— wondered was any one of the other sixteen gazing at his cubicle and thinking, realising as he was: nothing. He realised that he would never know.

Nothing. Or almost nothing. He looked down at his body: thin belly, thin arms, a limp member. He knew he had arrived at the point where he would masturbate. He always came to this point in different ways, with different thoughts, by different stages. But when he had reached it, he always realised that the ways had been similar, the ways had been the same way, only the phrasing different. And he began then, taking himself with both hands, caressing himself with a familiar, bleak motion, knowing that afterwards the bleakness would only be intensified after the brief distraction of feeling—in this like everything—observing the while the motion of his belly muscles, glistening under their sheen of running water. And as he felt the mechanical surge of desire run through him he heard the splashing of an anonymous body in the cubicle adjacent. The thought came to him that somebody could be watching him. But no, he thought then, almost disappointed, who could, working at himself harder. He was standing when he felt an exultant muscular thrill run through him, arching his back, straining his calves upwards, each toe pressed passionately against the tiled floor.

The young Trinidadian in the next cubicle squeezed out a sachet of lemon soft shampoo and rubbed it to a lather between two brown palms. Flecks of sawdust—he was an apprentice carpenter—mingled with the snow-white foam. He pressed two handfuls of it under each bicep, ladled it across his chest and belly and rubbed it till the foam seethed and melted to the colour of dull whey, and the water swept him clean again, splashed his body back to its miraculous brown and he slapped each nipple laughingly in turn and thought of a clean body under a crisp shirt, of a night of love under a low red-lit roof, of the thumping symmetry of a reggae band.

There was one intense moment of silence. He was standing, spent, sagging. He heard:

"Hey, you rass, not finished yet?"

"How'd I be finished?"

"Well move that corpse, rassman. Move!"

He watched the seed that had spattered the tiles be swept by the shower-water, diluting its grey, ultimately vanishing into the fury of current round the plug-hole. And he remembered the curving cement wall of his childhood and the spent tide and the rocks and the dried green stretches of sea-lettuce and because the exhaustion was delicious now and bleak, because he knew there would never be anything but that exhaustion after all the fury of effort, all the expense of passion and shame, he walked through the green-rose curtain and took the cut-throat razor from his pack and went back to the shower to cut his wrists. And dying, he thought of nothing more significant than the way, the way he had come here, of the green bridge and the bowed figure under the brick wall and the facade of the Victorian bath-house, thinking: there is nothing more significant.

Of the dozen or so people who gathered to stare—as people will—none of them thought: "Why did he do it?" All of them, pressed into a still, tight circle, staring at the shiplike body, knew intrinsically. And a middle-aged, fat and possibly simple negro phrased the thought:

"Every day the Lord send me I think I do that. And every day the Lord send me I drink bottle of wine and forget 'bout doin' that."

They took with them three memories: the memory of a thin, almost hairless body with reddened wrists; the memory of a thin, finely-wrought razor whose bright silver was mottled in places with rust; and the memory of a spurting shower-nozzle, an irregular drip of water. And when they emerged to the world of bright afternoon streets they saw the green-painted iron bridge and the red-brick wall and knew it to be in the nature of these, too, that the body should act thus—

Seduction

"YOU DON'T believe me, do you," he said, "you don't believe anything, but I've seen her"—and he repeated it again, but I didn't have to listen this time, I could imagine it so vividly. The naked woman's clothes lying in a heap under the drop from the road where the beach was clumsy with rocks and pebbles, her fat body running on the sand at the edge of the water, the waves splashing round her thick ankles. The imagining was just like the whole summer, it throbbed with forbidden promise. I had been back in the town two days and each day we had hung around till twilight, when the hours seemed longest, when the day would extend its dying till it seemed ready to burst, the sky like a piece of stretched gauze over it, grey, melancholy, yet infinitely desirable and unknown. This year I was a little afraid of him, though he was still smaller than me. I envied and loved his pointed shoes that were turned up and scuffed white and his hair that curled and dripped with oil that did its best to contain it in a duck's tail. I loved his assurance, the nonchalant way he let the vinegar run from the chip-bag onto the breast of his off-white shirt. But I kept all this quiet knowing there were things he envied about me too. I think each of us treasured this envy, longing to know how the other had changed but disdaining to ask. We loved to talk in monosyllables conscious of the other's envy, a hidden mutual delight underneath it like blood. Both of us stayed in the same guest-house as last year. My room faced the sea, his the grounds of the convent, the basket-ball pitch with the tennis-net running through it where the nuns swung rackets with brittle, girlish laughter. We sniffed the smell of apples that came over the town from the monastery

orchard behind it and the smell of apples in late August meant
something different to me this year, as did the twilight. Last year
it would have meant an invitation to rob. I wondered did it mean
the same to him. I concluded that it must, with his hair like that.
But then he was tougher, more obscene.

"Look, she's coming out now." He nodded his head sideways
towards the chip-shop and I stared in through the dripping
steamed glass. It looked warm inside, warm and greasy. I saw
the woman coming out of the tiny corridor in which the chips
were fried, leaning against the steel counter. Some older boys
waiting for orders threw jibes at her. She laughed briefly, then
took out a cigarette, put it in her mouth and lit it. I knew that
when the cigarette came out its tip would be covered in lipstick,
the way it happens in films. When she took the coins from them
two gold bangles slipped down onto her fat wrist. There was
something mysterious, hard and tired about her, some secret
behind those layers of make-up which those older boys shared.
I watched them laughing and felt the hard excitement of the
twilight, the apples. And I believed him then, though I knew
how much he lied. I believed him because I wanted to believe it,
to imagine it, the nakedness of this fat blonde woman who
looked older than her twenty-five years, who sang every Saturday night at the dance in the local hotel.

"Leanche's her name. Leanche the lion."

"Lioness," I said, being the erudite one. He looked at me and
spat.

"When'll you ever dry up." I spat too. "Here." He held out
the chip bag.

I took one. It was like when I came to the guest-house and he
had already been there a day. He stood in the driveway pulling
leaves off the rhododendron bush as we took things off the rack
of our Ford car. I looked over at him, the same as last year, but
with a new sullenness in his face. I hoped my face was even more
deadpan. He turned his face away when I looked but stayed still,
pulling the oily leaves till the unpacking was finished. Then I

went over to talk to him. He said that the town was a dump this year, that there was an Elvis playing in the local cinema. He said that Ford cars with high backs had gone out since the ark. I asked him had his people got a car yet and he said no. But somehow it seemed worse to have a car with a high back and rusted doors than no car at all. He said, "Come on, we'll go to the town," and we both walked to the gate, to the road that ran from the pier towards the town where every house was painted white and yellow and in summer was a guest-house.

"Let's go inside," he said, just as it was getting dark and the last of the queue filed from the chipper. "We've no money," I said. "Anyway, I don't believe you." I hoped my fright didn't glare through. "It's true," he said. "The man in the cinema told me." "Did he see her," I asked. "No, his brother did." There was disdain in the statement that I couldn't have countered.

We pushed open the glass door, he took out a comb as he was doing so and slicked it through his hair. I went over to the yellow jukebox and pushed idly at the buttons. "Are ye puttin' money in it, son," I heard. I turned and saw her looking at me, the ridiculously small curls of her hair tumbling round her large face. Her cheeks were red and her dress was low and her immense bosom showed white through it, matching the grease-stains on her apron. "No," I said and began to blush to the roots, "we just wanted to know . . ."

"Have you got the time," Jamie burst in. "Have you eyes in your head," she countered. She raised her arm and pointed to a clock in the wall above her. Twenty past ten.

We had walked past the harbour and the chip-shop and the Great Northern Hotel that were all the same as last year. The rich hotelier's son who had left the priesthood and had gone a little mad was on the beach again, turning himself to let his stomach get the sun now that his back was brown. Jamie told me about the two Belfast sisters who wore nylons and who were Protestants, how they sat in the cinema every night waiting for something. He asked me had I ever got anything off a girl that wore nylons. I asked him had he. He said nothing, but spat on the ground and stirred the spittle with the sole of his shoe. The difference in the town was bigger now, lurid, hemming us in. I borrowed his comb and slicked it through my hair but my hair refused to quiff, it fell back each time on my forehead, incorrigibly flat and sandy-coloured.

The woman in the chip-shop smiled and crooked her arm on the counter, resting her chin on her fist. The folds of fat bulged round the golden bangles. "Anything else you'd like to know." I felt a sudden mad urge to surpass myself, to go one better than Jamie's duck-tailed hair. "Yeah," I began, "do you . . ." Then I stopped. She had seemed a little like an idiot to me but something more than idiocy stopped me. "Do I!" she said and turned her head towards me, looking at me straight in the eyes. And in the green irises underneath the clumsy mascara there was a mocking light that frightened me. I thought of the moon with a green mist around it like the Angel of Death in *The Ten Commandments*. I saw her cheeks and heard the wash of the sea and imagined her padding feet on the sand. And I shivered at the deeper, infinite idiocy there, the lurid idiocy that drew couples into long grass to engage in something I wasn't quite sure of. I blushed with shame, with longing to know it, but was saved by her banging hand on the silver counter. "If you don't want chips, hop it." "Don't worry," said Jamie, drawing the comb through his hair. "Don't worry," I said, listening to his hair click oilily, making for the glass door. "I still don't believe you," I said to him outside. "Do you want to wait up and see then." I didn't answer. Jamie drew a series of curves that formed a naked woman in the window-dew. We both watched them drip slowly into a mess of watery smudges.

We had gone to the cinema that first night, through the yellow-emulsioned doorway into the darkness of the long hall, its windows covered with sheets of brown paper. I smelt the smells of last year, the sweaty felt brass of the seats and the dust rising from the aisle to be changed into diamonds by the cone of light above. There was a scattering of older couples there, there was Elvis on the screen, on a beach in flowered bathing-trunks, but no Belfast sisters. "Where are they," I asked him, with the ghost of a triumphant note in my voice. He saved himself by taking out a butt, lighting it and pulling harshly on it. We drank in Elvis silently. Later the cinema projectionist put his head between both our shoulders and said, "Hey boys, you want to see the projection-room?" His breath smelt the same as last year, of cigarettes and peppermint. But this year we said no.

Later again I sat in my room and watched the strand, where two nuns were swinging tennis-rackets on a court they had scrawled on the sand. It was ten past nine and the twilight was well advanced, the balance between blue and grey almost perfect. I sat on my bed and pulled my knees to my chest, rocking softly, listening to the nuns' tinkling laughter, staring at the billows their habits made with each swing of their arms. Soon even the nuns left and the strand was empty but for the scrawled tennis-court and the marks of their high-heeled boots. But I watched on, hearing the waves break, letting the light die in the room around me, weeping for the innocence of last year.

We pressed ourselves against the wall below the road, trying to keep our feet from slipping off the large round pebbles. My father was calling my name from the drive of the guest-house. His voice seemed to echo right down the beach, seeming worried and sad. Soon even the echo died away and Jamie clambered up and peeped over the top and waved to me that no-one was there. Then we walked down the strand making a long trail of footsteps in the half-light. We settled ourselves behind an upturned boat and began to wait. We waited for hours, till Jamie's face became pinched and pale, till my teeth began to chatter. He stared at the sea and broke the teeth from his comb, one by one, scattering them at his feet. I spat in the sand and watched how my spittle rolled into tiny sandballs. The sea washed and sucked and washed and sucked but remained empty of fat women. Then Jamie began to talk, about kisses with the mouth open and closed, about the difference between the feel of a breast under and over a jumper, between nylons and short white socks. He talked for what seemed hours and after a while I stopped listening, I knew he was lying anyway. Then suddenly I noticed he had stopped talking. I didn't know how long he had stopped, but I knew it had been some time before I noticed it. I turned and saw he was hunched up, his face blank like a child's. All the teeth were broken from his comb, his hand was clutching it insensibly and he was crying softly. His hair was wild with curls, the oil was dripping onto his forehead, his lips were purple with the cold. I touched him on the elbow and when his quiet sobbing didn't stop I took off my coat and put it gingerly round his shoulders. He shivered and moved in close to me and his head touched my chest and lay there. I held him there while he slept, thinking how much smaller than me he was after all.

There was a thin rim of light round the edge of the sea when he woke. His face was pale, though not as grey as that light, and his teeth had begun to chatter. "What happened," he asked, shaking my coat off. "You were asleep," I said, "you missed it," and began a detailed account of how the woman had begun running from the pier right up past me to the end of the strand, how her breasts had bobbed as the water splashed round her thick ankles. "Liar," he said. "Yes," I said. Then I thought of home. "What are we going to do?" I asked him. He rubbed his eyes with his hand and drew wet smudges across each cheek. Then he got up and began to walk towards the sea. I followed him, knowing the sea would obliterate his tears and any I might have. When he came near the water he began to run, splashing the waves round him with his feet and I ran too, but with less abandon, and when he fell face down in the water I fell too. When I could see him through the salt water he was laughing madly in a crying sort of way, ducking his head in and out of the water the way swimmers do. I got to my feet and tried to pull him up but his clothes were clinging to every bone of his thin body. Then I felt myself slipping, being pulled from the legs and

I fell in the water again and I felt his arms around my waist, tightening, the way boys wrestle, but more quietly then, and I felt his body not small any longer, pressing against mine. I heard him say "this is the way lovers do it" and felt his mouth on my neck but I didn't struggle, I knew that in the water he couldn't see my tears or see my smile.

Sand

THE DONKEY'S hooves were like his sister's fingernails, long and pointed. Except for the ends, which were splintered and rough, not fine and hard.

He was sitting on it, trying to make it move. He could feel its spine against the bone between his legs. He could feel its flanks, like two soft sweaty cushions against each knee and thigh.

He dug his heel into one of the flanks and it shifted a few feet.

"Stop kicking up sand," his sister said. She had that annoyed tone in her voice.

"Will you come for a swim if I stop," he asked.

"Oh just stop, would you."

"No," he said.

He kicked at the donkey again, though he dreaded his sister's tongue. When she spoke she seemed to know so much that he didn't. It was like her suntan lotion, like her habit of lying by the sea with her eyes closed, on their towel. He felt that somewhere he knew as much as she, but when he came to say it he could never find the words.

"If you kick more sand at me—"

"All right," he said. "All right."

He put his hands on the donkey's neck and wondered how he could get down with some dignity, some of her dignity. He looked at the dark blue of the sea and the light blue of the sky, thinking about this. Then he heard something far away behind him. A shout. He turned on the donkey, saw someone running across the burrows, arms waving.

He clambered down quickly, without dignity. He thought of tinkers. He knew most donkeys belonged to tinkers. He looked

at this donkey and it was as impassive as ever, its hooves curling
out of the white sand.

The figure came nearer, running with a peculiar adult single-
mindedness. It wasn't an adult however, it was a boy, not much
older than him. The boy had run beyond the rim of the grass
now and was kicking up sand. He was totally naked. He held a
boot in one hand with which every now and then he covered his
genitals.

But mostly he couldn't cover them, his arms flailing as he ran.
And the boy saw the naked figure, smaller than him, but
stronger and much browner, jogging to a halt. He saw the open
mouth panting and the eyes, wary as his were, but older and
angrier than his could ever have been. The brown nakedness
stopping at the waist becoming grey-white nakedness. The boot
stationary now in front of the patch of hair.

"That's my donkey. Leave hold of it."

He did so immediately. Not because he was afraid, which he
was, but because he would have done anything those eyes asked.
He looked at the shoe and it didn't quite hide that curl of angry
hair and that sex. He looked at his sister. She was looking the
other way, blushing, arched rigid in her blue swimsuit.

"I'll give you that the next time."

A small bony fist hovered before his face. Behind it were the
eyes, young as his, but with clusters of ancient wrinkles round
the edges.

"Okay," he said. He tried not to sound defeated. And the
tinker turned and pulled the donkey after him by the thin hair
on its neck.

"Really," his sister said.

And now he blushed. The tinker was on the burrows now,
pulling the donkey by the hair on its neck. His buttocks swung
as he walked, two white patches against the brown of his thin
body.

He felt blamed for that nakedness. He felt he could hate his
sister, for blaming him.

"Really," she said. "Some people."

He felt the words were false, picked up from grown-ups. Her body was arched forward now towards her drawn-up knees, her arms were placed across her knees and her chin was resting on her arms. Her eyelids were lowered, not quite closed, but sealing him off. He wanted to say sorry, but her eyes lay between him and his words. Then he did hate her. He hated her in a very basic way, he felt he would tear her apart, the way one tears the many wrappings off the parcel in the pass-the-parcel game, to see what's inside. He didn't know whether he'd hate what would be inside.

"Jean—" he began, but she turned on her stomach, away from him, exposing her long back to the sun.

He heard a shout behind him and he turned, glad to escape her. He saw the tinker waving his hands some distance down in the burrows, shouting something he couldn't hear. There was something urgent about him, flailing hands against the sky. So he walked, even though he was afraid, leaving his sister with her cheek resting on her linked hands.

As he walked the tinker grew bigger and the flailing gradually stopped. There was the hot feel of the sand under his bare feet, then the feel of grass, whistling by his calves. Then the boy was in front of him, arms on his hips, waiting for him to approach. He was wearing men's trousers now, sizes too big for him.

"You want a go on the donkey."

He nodded dumbly.

"I'll give you half an hour with the donkey for half an hour with your sister."

The boy began to laugh at the thought, his sister and the donkey, an even swop. The tinker began to laugh too and that made the boy laugh louder, huge laughs that went right through his body and stretched his stomach-muscles tight. The tinker's laugh was softer, more knowledgeable. The boy heard this and stopped and looked into the blue eyes which wrinkled in some complicity and kept laughing. Then the boy began to laugh again, loving his laughter, the way he sometimes laughed when adults were laughing. The joke had changed into another joke, a joke he didn't understand, but that made it all the more funny.

Then the tinker stopped suddenly. He cupped his hands together to make a stirrup and held them out.

"Here."

The hands were grimy and lined, skin flaking off them. The boy felt compliant. He was opening a box to let the winds out. He knew and he didn't know. He placed his left foot in the stirrup of flaking hands and swung onto the donkey and the tinker's foot kicked the donkey and the donkey ran.

He was holding its neck, fearful and exhilarated. It was running like he didn't know donkeys could run with rapid thumps of hoof off the grass, with its spine, hard as a gate, crashing off his groin. He pressed his head against its neck and could hear its breathing, angry and sullen, thumping with its hooves. His knees clutched the swollen belly and his hands, gripping each other under the neck, were wet and slimy with saliva from the open jaw. His eyes were closed and he saw in the black behind his eyelids something even blacker emerging, whorling and retreating again.

Then it stopped. He slid over its head and fell to the ground. He fell flat out, his cheek against the burrows' grass and heard his sister screaming, a clear scream, clear as silver.

The donkey's head was hanging and its sides were heaving. Between its legs a black erection dangled, heaving with its sides. The scream still echoed in the boy's mind. Clear and silver, speaking to him, like the reflection of sun on sea-water. He ran.

He ran faster than the donkey. He saw the green burrows, then the white sand, then the clear blue of his sister's swimsuit, then a browned tanned back. The sand was kicking up in clumps around him as he threw himself on that back.

He felt the naked shoulders under his hand. Then he felt the shoulders twisting and a hard body pushing him downwards, something hot, hard against his stomach. Both of their fists were hitting the other's face until he was hit hard, once and twice and they both, as if by mutual decision, went quiet. He lay until he became conscious of the other's hot hard groin, then squirmed away. He looked up at his sister. Her head was in one hand and the other hand was covering the bare skin above her swimsuit. He heard a rustle of sand and heard the tinker boy getting up.

"I thought we'd made a swop." There was a spot of blood on his wizened mouth. He bent forward as if to strike again but changed his hand's direction just as rapidly and scratched the hair behind his ear. The boy started. He grinned.

"I'd only put it through you," he said. Then he hitched up his falling trousers and walked towards the grass.

When he got there he turned.

"That's the last you'll see of my donkey," he said. Then he chuckled with infinite sarcasm. "Unless you've got another sister." And he turned again and walked through the grass towards the donkey.

She was crying, great breathful sobs.

"You won't—" he asked.

"I will," she said. "I'll tell it all—"

The boy knew, however, that she would be ashamed. He picked up her towel and her suntan lotion and began to walk. He had forgotten about his hate. He was thinking of the donkey and the tinker's flaking palms and his sister's breasts. After a while he turned.

"Stop crying, will you. Nothing happened, did it."

His hands were wet with the donkey's saliva and to the saliva a fine film of sand was clinging. When he moved his fingers it rustled, whispered, sang.

Mr Solomon Wept

T HE CHILD had rolled pennies and the dodgem wheels had smoked for half a morning when Mr Solomon took time off to stand by the strand. He stood where he was accustomed to, on the lip of the cement path that seemed designed to run right to the sea but that crumbled suddenly and inexplicably into the sand. Mr Solomon smoked a cigarette there, holding it flatly between his lips, letting the smoke drift over his thin moustache into his nostrils. His eyes rested on the lumps of rough-cast concrete half-embedded in the sand. His breath came in with a soft, scraping sound.

The sea looked warm and lazy in midday. Down the beach a marquee was being erected. Mr Solomon looked at the people on the beach, the sunbathers and the men who were unwinding the marquee canvas. He wore a brown suit with narrow legs and wide lapels, his thin face looked like it was long accustomed to viewing sunbathers, people on beaches. Mr Solomon then stopped looking at the people and looked at the sea. He took the cigarette from his mouth, inhaled and replaced it again. The sea looked dark blue to him, the colour of midnight rather than of midday. And though it looked flat and indolent and hot, its blueness was clear and sharp, a sharpness emphasised by the occasional flurry of white foam, the slight swell far out. Mr Solomon knew these to be white horses. But today they reminded him of lace, lace he imagined round a woman's throat, a swelling bosom underneath, covered in navy cloth. He had seen an advertisement for sherry once with such a picture. He saw her just under the sea, just beneath the film of glassblue. If he lifted his eyes to the horizon again the sea became flat and indolent, and probably too hot for swimming.

Mr Solomon lifted his eyes and saw the flat sea and the flat yellow strand. He thought of the child he had left, something morose and forlorn about the way he pushed penny after penny into the metal slot. Then he looked down the strand and saw the large marquee pole being hoisted and only then realised that it was Race day. And Mr Solomon remembered the note again, he remembered the nights of surprised pain, the odd gradual feeling of deadness, how before it happened it had been unthinkable and how after it happened somehow anything other than it had become unthinkable. Now he dressed the boy, shopped, the boy sat in the change booth staring at the racing page while he drank in the Northern Star over lunchtime. He remembered how his wife had left him on Race day, one year ago. How he had come to Laytown three days before the races, to catch the crowds. How on the fourth day he had gone to the caravan behind the rifle-range and found it empty, a note on the flap table. Its message was hardly legible, though simple. Gone with Chas. Won't have to hate you any more. He remembered how he had wondered who Chas was, how he had sat on the unmade bed and stared at this note that over the length of the first night assumed the significance of a train ticket into a country he had never heard of. For he had long ceased to think of her with the words love or hate, he had worked, rolled his thin cigarettes, she had totted the books while he supervised the rent, those words were like the words school or god, part of a message that wasn't important any more, a land that was far away. And now he saw the note and thought of the world that had lived for her, thought of the second May, the May behind the one that woke first beside him in the cramped white caravan, that was sitting beside the singing kettle when he woke; this was Chas's May—but it mightn't have been Chas, it could have spelt Chad—and the thought that she existed gave him a feeling of surprised pain, surprise at the May he had never known of, surprise at the loss of what he had never possessed. But after three days the pained surprise had died and a new surprise asserted itself—a surprise at how easily the unthinkable became possible. He found it was easy to cook, to tot the books, to supervise the dodgem tracks and shooting-range all in one. The boy helped him, he watched the boy from behind the glass of the change booth emptying the slot-machines. When the races finished he stayed on, found the move to another holiday-spot too much bother and unnecessary anyway, since less money would do now. Even when the season ended he didn't move, he sat in the draughty amusement hall through winter and made more than enough to keep rolling his thin cigarettes. The rusted slot-machines became a focus for the local youths with sullen faces and greased hair and he found forgetting her almost as easy a task as that of living with her had been. She had been shrewish, he told himself as her memory grew dimmer, her hair had often remained unwashed for days, she would have soon, within the year, gone to fat. Thus he killed the memory of another her neatly, he forgot the nights at the Palais in Brighton, the evenings in the holiday pubs, her platinum hair and the rich dark of the bottled Guinness (a ladies' drink then) tilted towards her laughing mouth.

But he saw the marquee pole stagger upright and suddenly remembered her as if she had died and as if the day of the Laytown Races was her anniversary. He saw the white horses whip and the marquee canvas billow round the pole and thought suddenly of the dress she had called her one good dress with its sad lace frills and the bodice of blue satin that had more restitchings than original threads. A sense of grief came over him, a feeling of quiet sadness, not wholly unpleasing. He began to think of her as if she had died, he thought of the woman who had lived with him and who indeed had died. He imagined flowers for her, dark blood-red roses, and felt bleak and clean as if in celebration of her imagined death he was somehow cleansing both him and his image of her.

He lit another cigarette and turned back on the cement path. He passed a family coming from an ice-cream van a little down it, the cones in their hands already sodden. Mr Solomon watched them pass him and felt he had a secret safe, totally safe from them. He felt as if there was a hidden flame inside him, consuming him, while the exterior remained the same as ever, the smoke still drifted over the same thin lip. He passed the green corrugated hall that served as a golf-club and remembered how each year they came through she had got him to pay green fees, how they had both made an afternoon's slow crawl over nine holes. How she had longed to be someday, a proper member in a proper club. "But we never settle down enough, do we, Jimmy, 'cept in winter, when it's too wet to play . . ."

Mr Solomon walked down the cement walk away from the beach and the rising marquee and felt his grief inside him like old port, hot and mellow. He came to the tarmac road and stood, staring at the tottering facade of the amusements and the dull concrete front of the Northern Star opposite. He wavered for one moment and then headed for the brass-studded door of the Northern Star, the mute lights and wood-and-brass fittings being like night to him at first until his eyes settled. He ordered a drink and gave the barman a sharp look before downing it.

"This one's for my wife," he said.

"I didn't know you had one," said the barman, who was always courteous.

"In memory of her. She died last year."

"I'm sorry," said the barman. "Her anniversary?"

"Died on Race day," began Mr Solomon but by this time the barman had headed off discreetly for a customer at the other end. He blinked once then finished his drink and began to feel very angry at the courteous barman. He felt the whiskey tickle down his throat, he felt something in him had been sullied by the bland courtesy, the discreet lights of the hotel bar. He left.

Outside the brightness blinded him as much as the darkness had before. Mr Solomon stared down the lean yellow street. It was packed with people and as he watched them, Mr Solomon began to feel for the first time a hatred towards them, en masse. He felt a malignant sameness in them. He felt they laughed, in their summer clothes. He felt they didn't know, in their summer clothes. He felt like a cog in the mechanism of holidays, of holiday towns, he felt somehow slave to their bright clothes and suntans. He no longer felt she had died, he felt something had killed her, that impersonal holiday gaiety had enslaved them both, had aged him, like a slow cancerous growth, had annihilated her. He felt his grief burning inside now, like a rough Irish whiskey. He crossed the street a little faster than he normally did, though his walk was still lethargic by the street's standards. He went into the pub with the black-and-white gabled roof.

That afternoon his tale competed with the banjo-playing tinker, with the crack of beer-glasses, with the story of the roadworker's son who returned and bought out three local publicans. Mr Solomon shouted it, wept it, crowed with it, nobody listened, his thin face acquired a weasel look, a sorry look, his eyes grew more glazed and his speech more blurred, the reason for his grief grew hazy and indeterminate. By half-past four he was just drunk, all he knew was there was something somewhere to feel sorry over, profoundly sorry, somewhere a pain, though the reason for it he could no longer fathom, nor why it should be his pain particularly. Why not that Meath farmer's, with the flushed face and the tweed suit, and at this Mr Solomon grew offensive, sloppily offensive and found himself removed.

He went through the hard daylight again into the dark of the Amusement Parlour. He heard a rustle in the left-hand corner and saw the boy starting up guiltily from the peepshow machine. Mr Solomon thought of the near-naked starlets in high-heels and out-of-date hairdos and got angry again. "I told you never to go near that," he rasped. The boy replied with a swift obscenity that shocked him silent. He could only stare, at his home-made cloth anorak, his hair clumsily quiffed, sticking out in places, his thin impenetrable face. At his son's face, new to him because he'd never seen it. He made to move towards him, only then realising how drunk he was. He saw the boy's hand draw

back and an object fly from it. He raised his hand to protect his
face and felt something strike his knuckles. He heard the coin
ring off the cement floor and the boy's footsteps running towards the door. He ran after him drunkenly, shouting.

The boy ran towards the beach. Mr Solomon followed. He
saw the horses thunder on the beach, distorted by his drunken
run. He saw the line of sand they churned up, the sheets of spray
they raised when they galloped in the tide. He saw the boy
running for the marquee.

Mr Solomon could hear a brass band playing. He ran till he
could run no longer and then he went forward in large clumsy
steps, dragging the sand as he went. The sound of the reeds and
trumpets grew clearer as he walked, repeated in one poignant
phrase, right down the beach. Mr Solomon came to a crowd
then, pressed round the marquee and began to push his way
desperately through it. He felt people like a wall against him,
forcing him out. He began to moan aloud, scrabbling at the
people in front of him to force his way in. He imagined the boy
at the centre of that crowd, playing a clear golden trumpet. He
could see the precise curve of the trumpet's mouth, the pumping
keys, the boy's expressionless eyes. He began to curse, trying to
wedge himself between the bodies, there was something desperate and necessary beyond them.

He felt himself lifted then, carried a small distance off and
thrown in the sand. He lifted his face and wept in the sand and
saw the horses churning the sea-spray into a wide area down by
the edge. He heard a loud cheer, somewhere behind him.

Night in Tunisia

T HAT YEAR they took the green house again. She was there again, older than him and a lot more venal. He saw her on the white chairs that faced the tennis-court and again in the burrows behind the tennis-court and again still down on the fifteenth hole where the golf-course met the mouth of the Boyne. It was twilight each time he saw her and the peculiar light seemed to suspend her for an infinity, a suspended infinite silence, full of years somehow. She must have been seventeen now that he was fourteen. She was fatter, something of an exhausted woman about her and still something of the girl whom adults called mindless. It was as if a cigarette between her fingers had burnt towards the tip without her noticing. He heard people talking about her even on her first day there, he learnt that underneath her frayed blouse her wrists were marked. She was a girl about whom they would talk anyway since she lived with a father who drank, who was away for long stretches in England. Since she lived in a green corrugated-iron house. Not even a house, a chalet really, like the ones the townspeople built to house summer visitors. But she lived in it all the year round.

THEY TOOK A green house too that summer, also made of corrugated iron. They took it for two months this time, since his father was playing what he said would be his last stint, since there was no more place for brassmen like him in the world of three-chord showbands. And this time the two small bedrooms were divided differently, his sister taking the small one, since she had to dress on her own now, himself and his father sharing the larger one where two years ago his sister and he had slept. Every night his father took the tenor sax and left for Mosney to play with sixteen others for older couples who remembered what the big bands of the forties sounded like. And he was left alone with his sister who talked less and less as her breasts grew bigger. With the alto saxophone which his father said he could learn when he forgot his fascination for three-chord ditties. With the guitar which he played a lot, as if in spite against the alto saxophone. And with the broken-keyed piano which he played occasionally.

When it rained on the iron roof the house sang and he was reminded of a green tin drum he used to hand when he was younger. It was as if he was inside it.

HE WANDERED round the first three days, his sister formal and correct beside him. There was one road made of tarmac, running through all the corrugated houses towards the tennis-court. It was covered always with drifts of sand, which billowed while they walked. They passed her once, on the same side, like an exotic and dishevelled bird, her long yellow cardigan coming down to her knees, covering her dress, if she wore any. He stopped as she passed and turned to face her. Her feet kept billowing up the sand, her eyes didn't see him, they were puffy and covered in black pencil. He felt hurt. He remembered an afternoon three years ago when they had lain on the golf-links, the heat, the nakedness that didn't know itself, the grass on their three backs.

"Why don't you stop her?" he asked his sister.

"Because," she answered. "Because, because."

HE BECAME OBSESSED with twilights. Between the hour after tea when his father left and the hour long after dark when his father came home he would wait for them, observe them, he would taste them as he would a sacrament. The tincture of the light fading, the blue that seemed to be sucked into a thin line beyond the sea into what the maths books called infinity, the darkness falling like a stone. He would look at the long shadows of the burrows on the strand and the long shadows of the posts that held the sagging tennis-nets on the tarmac courts. He would watch his sister walking down the road under the eyes of boys that were a little older than him. And since he hung around at twilight and well into the dark he came to stand with them, on the greens behind the clubhouse, their cigarette-tips and their laughter punctuating the dark. He played all the hits on the honky-tonk piano in the clubhouse for them and this compensated for his missing years. He played and he watched, afraid to say too much, listening to their jokes and their talk about girls, becoming most venal when it centred on her.

HE LAUGHED with them, that special thin laugh that can be stopped as soon as it's begun.

THERE WAS A raft they would swim out to on the beach. His skin was light and his arms were thin and he had no Adam's apple to speak of, no hair creeping over his togs, but he would undress all the same with them and swim out. They would spend a day on it while the sun browned their backs and coaxed beads of resin from the planks. When they shifted too much splinters of wood shot through their flesh. So mostly they lay inert, on their stomachs, their occasional erections hidden beneath them, watching on the strand the parade of life.

IT GALLED HIS father what he played.

"What galls me," he would say, "is that you could be so good."

But he felt vengeful and played them incessantly and even sang the tawdry lyrics. Some day soon, he sang, I'm going to tell the Moon about the crying game. And maybe he'll explain, he sang.

"WHY DON'T YOU speak to her?" he asked his sister when they passed her again. It was seven o'clock and it was getting dark.

"Because," she said. "Because I don't."

But he turned. He saw her down the road, her yellow cardigan making a scallop round her fattening buttocks.

"Rita," he called. "Rita."

She turned. She looked at him blankly for a moment and then she smiled, her large pouting lips curving the invitation she gave to any boy that shouted at her.

HE SAT AT THE broken-keyed piano. The light was going down over the golf-links and his sister's paperback novel was turned over on the wooden table. He heard her in her room, her shoes knocking off the thin wooden partition. He heard the rustling of cotton and nylon and when the rustles stopped for a moment he got up quickly from the piano and opened the door. She gave a gasp and pulled the dress from the pile at her feet to cover herself. He asked her again did she remember and she said she didn't and her face blushed with such shame that he felt sorry and closed the door again.

THE SEA HAD the movement of cloth but the texture of glass. It flowed and undulated, but shone hard and bright. He thought of cloth and glass and how to mix them. A cloth made of glass fibre or a million woven mirrors. He saw that the light of twilight was repeated or reversed at early morning.

HE DECIDED to forget about his sister and join them, the brashness they were learning, coming over the transistors, the music that cemented it. And the odd melancholy of the adulthood they were about to straddle, to ride like a Honda down a road with one white line, pointless and inevitable.

HIS FATHER on his nights off took out his Selmer, old loved talisman that was even more shining than on the day he bought it. He would sit and accompany while his father stood and played—"That Certain Feeling," "All the Things You Are," the names that carried their age with them, the embellishments and the filled-in notes that must have been something one day but that he had played too often, that he was too old now to get out of. And to please his father he would close his eyes and play, not knowing how or what he played and his father would stop and let him play on, listening. And he would occasionally look and catch that look in his listening eyes, wry, sad and loving, his pleasure at how his son played only marred by the knowledge of how little it meant to him. And he would catch the look in his father's eyes and get annoyed and deliberately hit a bum note to spoil it. And the sadness in the eyes would outshine the wryness then and he would be sorry, but never sorry enough.

HE SOON LEARNT that they were as mistrustful of each other as he was of them and so he relaxed somewhat. He learnt to turn his silence into a pose. They listened to his playing and asked about his sister. They lay on the raft, watched women on the strand, their eyes stared so hard that the many shapes on the beach became one, indivisible. It made the sand-dunes and even the empty clubhouse redundant. Lying face down on the warm planks, the sun burning their backs with an aching languor. The blaring transistor, carried over in its plastic bag. Her on the beach, indivisible, her yellow cardigan glaring even on the hottest days. He noticed she had got fatter since he came. Under them on the warm planks the violent motions of their pricks. She who lived in the chalet all the year round.

THE ONE BEDROOM and the two beds, his father's by the door, his by the window. The rippled metal walls. The moon like water on his hands, the bed beside him empty. Then the front door opening, the sound of the saxophone case laid down. His eyes closed, his father stripping in the darkness, climbing in, long underwear and vest. The body he'd known lifelong, old and somewhat loved, but not like his Selmer, shining. They get better with age, he said about instruments. His breath scraping the air now, scraping over the wash of the sea, sleeping.

THE TALL THIN boy put his mouth to the mouth of the French letter and blew. It expanded, huge and bulbous, with a tiny bubble at the tip.

"It's getting worked up," he said.

He had dark curling hair and dark shaven cheeks and a mass of tiny pimples where he shaved. The pimples spread from his ears downwards, as if scattered from a pepper-canister. His eyes were dark too, and always a little closed.

"We'll let it float to England," he said, "so it can find a fanny big enough for it."

They watched it bobbing on the waves, brought back and forwards with the wash. Then a gust of wind lifted it and carried it off, falling to skim the surface and rising again, the bubble towards the sky.

HE HAD WALKED up from the beach and the French letter bound for England. He had seen her yellow cardigan on the tennis-court from a long way off, above the strand. He was watching her play now, sitting on the white wrought-iron seat, his hands between his legs.

She was standing on the one spot, dead-centre of the court, hardly looking at all at her opponent. She was hitting every ball cleanly and lazily and the sound that came from her racquet each time was that taut twang that he knew only came from a good shot. He felt that even a complete stranger would have known, from her boredom, her ease, that she lived in a holiday town with a tennis-court all the year round. The only sign of effort was the beads of sweat round her lips and the tousled blonde curls round her forehead. And every now and then when the man she was playing against managed to send a shot towards the sidelines, she didn't bother to follow it at all. She let the white ball bounce impotent towards the wire mesh.

He watched the small fat man he didn't recognise lose three balls for every ball won. He relished the spectacle of a fat man in whites being beaten by a bored teenage girl in sagging high-heels. Then he saw her throw her eyes upwards, throw her racquet down and walk from the court. The white ball rolled towards the wire mesh.

She sat beside him. She didn't look at him but she spoke as if she had known him those three years.

"You play him. I'm sick of it."

He walked across the court and his body seemed to glow with the heat generated by the slight touch of hers. He picked up the racquet and the ball, placed his foot behind the white line and threw the ball up, his eye on it, white, skewered against the blue sky. Then it came down and he heard the resonant twang as his racquet hit it and it went spinning into the opposite court but there was no-one there to take it. He looked up and saw the fat man and her walking towards a small white car. The fat man gestured her in and she looked behind at him once before she entered.

And as the car sped off towards Mornington he swore she waved.

The car was gone down the Mornington road. He could hear the pop-pop of the tennis-balls hitting the courts and the twang of them hitting the racquets as he walked, growing fainter. He walked along the road, past the tarmac courts and past the grass courts and past the first few holes of the golf-course which angled in a T round the tennis courts. He walked past several squares of garden until he came to his. It wasn't really a garden, a square of sand and scutch. He walked through the gate and up the path where the sand had been trodden hard to the green corrugated door. He turned the handle in the door, always left open. He saw the small square room, the sand fanning across the line from the doorstep, the piano with the sheet-music perched on the keys. He thought of the midday sun outside, the car with her in the passenger seat moving through it, the shoulders of the figure in the driver's seat. The shoulders hunched and fat, expressing something venal. He thought of the court, the white tennis ball looping between her body and his. Her body relaxed, vacant and easeful, moving the racquet so the ball flew where she wished. His body worried, worrying the whole court. He felt there was something wrong, the obedient ball, the running man. What had she lost to gain that ease, he wondered. He thought of all the jokes he had heard and of the act behind the jokes that none of those who told the jokes experienced. The innuendos and the charged words like the notes his father played, like the melodies his father willed him to play. The rich full twang as the ball met her racquet at the centre.

He saw the alto saxophone on top of the piano. He took it down, placed it on the table and opened the case. He looked at the keys, remembering the first lessons his father had taught him when it was new-bought, months ago. The keys unpressed, mother-of-pearl on gold, spotted with dust. He took out the ligature and fixed the reed in the mouthpiece. He put it between his lips, settled his fingers and blew. The note came out harsh and childish, as if he'd never learnt. He heard a shifting movement in the inside room and knew that he'd woken his father.

HE PUT THE instrument back quickly and made for the tiny bathroom. He closed the door behind him quietly, imagining his father's grey vest rising from the bed to the light of the afternoon sun. He looked into the mirror that closed on the cabinet where the medicine things were kept. He saw his face in the mirror looking at him, frightened, quick glance. Then he saw his face taking courage and looking at him full-on, the brown eyes and the thin fragile jawline. And he began to look at his eyes as directly as they looked at him.

"YOU WERE PLAYING," HIS father said, in the living room, in shirtsleeves, in uncombed afternoon hair, "the alto—"

"No," he said, going for the front door, "you were dreaming—"

———

AND ON THE raft the fat asthmatic boy, obsessed more than any with the theatre on the strand, talking about "it" in his lisping, mournful voice, smoking cigarettes that made his breath wheeze more. He had made classifications, rigid as calculus, meticulous as algebra. There were girls, he said, and women, and in between them what he termed lady, the lines of demarcation finely and inexorably drawn. Lady was thin and sat on towels, with high-heels and suntan-lotions, without kids. Woman was fat, with rugs and breasts that hung or bulged, with children. Then there were girls, his age, thin fat and middling, nyloned, short-stockinged—

HE LAY ON HIS stomach on the warm wood and listened to the fat boy talking and saw her walking down the strand. The straggling, uncaring walk that, he decided, was none of these or all of these at once. She was wearing flat shoes that went down at the heels with no stockings and the familiar cardigan that hid what could have classified her. She walked to a spot up the beach from the raft and unrolled the bundled towel from under her arm. Then she kicked off her shoes and pulled off her cardigan and wriggled out of the skirt her cardigan had hidden. She lay back on the towel in the yellow bathing suit that was too young for her, through which her body seemed to press like a butterfly already moulting in its chrysalis. She took a bottle then and shook it into her palm and began rubbing the liquid over her slack exposed body.

HE LISTENED to the fat boy talking about her—he was local too—about her father who on his stretches home came back drunk and bounced rocks off the tin roof, shouting "Hewer."
"What does that mean," he asked.
"Just that," said the asthmatic boy. "Rhymes with sure."

HE LOOKED AT her again from the raft, her slack stomach bent forward, her head on her knees. He saw her head lift and turn lazily towards the raft and he stood up then, stretching his body upwards, under what he imagined was her gaze. He dived, his body imagining itself suspended in air before it hit the water. Underwater he held his breath, swam through the flux of tiny bubbles, like crotchets before his open eyes.

"WHAT DID YOU say she was," he asked the fat boy, swimming back to the raft.

"Hewer," said the fat boy, more loudly.

He looked towards the strand and saw her on her back, her slightly plump thighs towards the sky, her hands shielding her eyes. He swam to the side of the raft then and gripped the wood with one hand and the fat boy's ankle with the other and pulled. The fat boy came crashing into the water and went down and when his head came up, gasping for asthmatic breath, he forced it down once more, though he didn't know what whore meant.

HIS FATHER WAS cleaning the alto when he came back.

"What does hewer mean," he asked his father.

His father stopped screwing in the ligature and looked at him, his old sideman's eyes surprised, and somewhat moral.

"A woman," he said, "who sells her body for monetary gain."

He stopped for a moment. He didn't understand.

"That's tautology," he said.

"What's that?" his father asked.

"It repeats," he said, and went into the toilet.

HE HEARD THE radio crackle over the sound of falling water and heard a rapid-fire succession of notes that seemed to spring from the falling water, that amazed him, so much faster than his father ever played, but slow behind it all, melancholy, like a river. He came out of the toilet and stood listening with his father. Who is that, he asked his father. Then he heard the continuity announcer say the name Charlie Parker and saw his father staring at some point between the wooden table and the wooden holiday-home floor.

HE PLAYED LATER on the piano in the clubhouse with the dud notes, all the songs, the trivial mythologies whose significance he had never questioned. It was as if he was fingering through his years and as he played he began to forget the melodies of all those goodbyes and heartaches, letting his fingers take him where they wanted to, trying to imitate that sound like a river he had just heard. It had got dark without him noticing and when finally he could just see the keys as question-marks in the dark, he stopped. He heard a noise behind him, the noise of somebody who has been listening, but who doesn't want you to know they are there. He turned and saw her looking at him, black in the square of light coming through the door. Her eyes were on his hands that were still pressing the keys and there was a harmonic hum tiny somewhere in the air. Her eyes rose to his face, unseeing and brittle to meet his hot, tense stare. He still remembered the rough feel of the tartan blanket over them, three of them, the grass under them. But her eyes didn't, so he looked everywhere but on them, on her small pinched chin, ridiculous under her large face, on the yellow linen dress that was ragged round her throat, on her legs, almost black from so much sun. The tiny hairs on them glistened with the light behind her. He looked up then and her eyes were still on his, keeping his fingers on the keys, keeping the chord from fading.

HE WAS OUT on the burrows once more, he didn't know how, and he met the thin boy. The thin boy sat down with him where they couldn't be seen and took a condom from his pocket and masturbated among the bushes. He saw how the liquid was caught by the antiseptic web, how the sand clung to it when the thin boy threw it, like it does to spittle.

———

HE LEFT THE thin boy and walked down the beach, empty now of its glistening bodies. He looked up at the sky, from which the light was fading, like a thin silver wire. He came to where the beach faded into the mouth of a river. There was a statue there, a Virgin with thin fingers towards the sea, her feet layered with barnacles. There were fishermen looping a net round the mouth. He could see the dim line of the net they pulled and the occasional flashes of white salmon. And as the boat pulled the net towards the shore he saw how the water grew violent with flashes, how the loose shoal of silver-and-white turned into a panting, open-gilled pile. He saw the net close then, the fishermen lifting it, the water falling from it, the salmon laid bare, glutinous, clinging, wet, a little like boiled rice.

HE IMAGINED the glistening bodies that littered the beach pulled into a net like that. He imagined her among them, slapping for space, panting for air, he heard transistors blare Da Doo Ron Ron, he saw suntan-lotion bottles crack and splinter as the Fisher up above pulled harder. He imagined his face like a lifeguard's, dark sidelocks round his muscular jaw, a megaphone swinging from his neck, that crackled.

HE SAW THE thin band of light had gone, just a glow off the sea now. He felt frightened, but forced himself not to run. He walked in quick rigid steps past the barnacled Virgin then and down the strand.

"TEN BOB FOR a touch with the clothes on. A pound without."
　　They were playing pontoon on the raft. He was watching the beach, the bodies thicker than salmon. When he heard the phrase he got up and kicked the dirt-cards into the water. He saw the Queen of Hearts face upwards in the foam. As they made for him he dived and swam out a few strokes.
　　"Cunts," he yelled from the water. "Cunts."

———————

ON THE BEACH the wind blew fine dry sand along the surface, drawing it in currents, a tide of sand.

HIS SISTER LAID the cups out on the table and his father ate with long pauses between mouthfuls. His father's hand paused, the bread quivering in the air, as if he were about to say something. He looked at his sister's breasts across a bowl of apples, half-grown fruits. The apples came from monks who kept an orchard. Across the fields, behind the house. He imagined a monk's hand reaching for the unplucked fruit, white against the swinging brown habit. For monks never sunbathed.

WHEN HE HAD finished he got up from the table and idly pressed a few notes on the piano.

"Why do you play that," his father asked. He was still at the table, between mouthfuls.

"I don't know," he said.

"What galls me," said his father, "is that you could be good."

He played a bit more of the idiotic tune that he didn't know why he played.

"If you'd let me teach you," his father said, "you'd be glad later on."

"Then why not wait till later on and teach me then."

"Because you're young, you're at the age. You'll never learn as well as now, if you let me teach you. You'll never feel things like you do now."

He began to play again in defiance and then stopped.

"I'll pay you," his father said.

HIS FATHER WOKE him coming in around four. He heard his wheezing breath and his shuffling feet. He watched the grey, metal-coloured light filling the room that last night had emptied it. He thought of his father's promise to pay him. He thought of the women who sold their bodies for monetary gain. He imagined all of them on the dawn golf-course, waking in their dew-

sodden clothes. He imagined fairways full of them, their monetary bodies covered with fine drops of water. Their dawn chatter
like birdsong. Where was that golf-course, he wondered. He
crept out of bed and into his clothes and out of the door, very
quietly. He crossed the road and clambered over the wire fence
that separated the road from the golf-course. He walked
through several fairways, across several greens, past several
fluttering pennants with the conceit in his mind all the time of
her on one green, asleep and sodden, several pound notes in her
closed fist. At the fourteenth green he saw that the dull metal
colour had faded into morning, true morning. He began to walk
back, his feet sodden from the dew.

HE WENT IN through the green corrugated door and put on a
record of the man whose playing he had first heard two days
ago. The man played "Night in Tunisia," and the web of notes
replaced the web that had tightened round his crown. The notes
soared and fell, dispelling the world around him, tracing a series
of arcs that seemed to point to a place, or if not a place, a state
of mind. He closed his eyes and let the music fill him and tried
to see that place. He could see a landscape of small hills, stretching to infinity, suffused in a yellow light that seemed to lap like
water. He decided it was a place you were always in, yet always
trying to reach, you walked towards all the time and yet never
got there, as it was always beside you. He opened his eyes and
wondered where Tunisia was on the Atlas. Then he stopped
wondering and reached up to the piano and took down the alto
saxophone and placed it on the table. He opened the case and
saw it gleaming in the light, new and unplayed. He knew he was
waking his father from the only sleep he ever got, but he didn't
care, imagining his father's pleasure. He heard him moving in
the bedroom then, and saw him come in, his hair dishevelled,
putting his shirt on. His father sat then, while he stood, listening
to the sounds that had dispelled the world. When it had finished
his father turned down the volume controls and took his fingers
and placed them on the right keys and told him to blow.

HE LEARNED the first four keys that day and when his father took his own instrument and went out to his work in Butlins he worked out several more for himself. When his father came back, at two in the morning, he was still playing. He passed him in the room, neither said anything, but he could feel his father's pleasure, tangible, cogent. He played on while his father undressed in the bedroom and when he was asleep he put it down and walked out the door, across the hillocks of the golf-course onto the strand, still humid with the warmth of that incredible summer.

HE FORGOT the raft and the games of pontoon and the thin boy's jargon. He stayed inside for days and laboriously transferred every combination of notes he had known on the piano onto the metal keys. He lost his tan and the gold sheen of the instrument became quickly tarnished with sweat, the sweat that came off his fingers in the hot metal room. He fashioned his mouth round the reed till the sounds he made became like a power of speech, a speech that his mouth was the vehicle for but that sprang from the knot of his stomach, the crook of his legs.

AS HE PLAYED he heard voices and sometimes the door knocked. But he turned his back on the open window and the view of the golf-course. Somewhere, he thought, there's a golf-course where bodies are free, not for monetary gain—

HE BROKE HIS habit twice. Once he walked across the fields to the orchard where the monks plucked fruit with white fingers. He sat on a crumbling wall and watched the darkening and fading shadows of the apple trees. Another night he walked back down the strand to where it faded into the river mouth. He looked at the salmonless water and imagined the lifeguard up above calling through his megaphone. He imagined childhood falling from him, coming off his palms like scales from a fish. He didn't look up, he looked down at his fingers that were forming hard coats of skin at the tips, where they touched the keys.

AND THEN, TEN days after it had started, his face in the mirror looked older to him, his skin paler, his chin more ragged, less round. His father got up at half-past three and played the opening bars of "Embraceable You" and instead of filling in while his father played, he played while his father filled in. And then they both played, rapidly, in a kind of mutual anger, through all his favourites into that area where there are no tunes, only patterns like water, that shift and never settle. And his father put his instrument away and put several pound notes on the table. He took them, put the case up above the piano and went out the green door.

IT WAS FIVE o'clock as he walked down the road by the golf-course, squinting in the sunlight. He walked down by the tennis-court onto the strand, but it was too late now and the beach was empty and there was no-one on the raft.

HE WALKED back with the pound notes hot in his pocket and met the fat boy with two racquets under his arm. The fat boy asked him did he want to play and he said, "Yes."

THEY HAD LOBBED an endless series of balls when the fat boy said, "Did you hear?" "Hear what," he asked and then the fat boy mentioned her name. He told him how the lifeguard had rescued her twice during the week, from a part of the beach too near the shore to drown in by accident. He hit the ball towards the fat boy and imagined her body in the lifeguard's arms, his mouth on her mouth, pushing the breath in. Then he saw her sitting on the wrought-iron seat in a green dress now, vivid against the white metal. The pound notes throbbed in his pocket, but he hadn't the courage to stop playing and go to the seat. Her eyes were following the ball as it went backwards and forwards, listless and vacant. The light gradually became grey, almost as grey as the ball, so in the end he could only tell where it fell by the sound and they missed more than half the volleys. But still she sat on the white chair, her eyes on the ball, following it forwards and back. He felt a surge of hope in himself. He would tell her about that place, he told himself, she doesn't know. When it got totally dark he would stop, he told himself, go to her. But he knew that it never gets totally dark and he just might never stop and she might never rise from the white seat.

HE HIT THE BALL way above the fat boy's head into the wire meshing. He let the racquet fall on the tarmac. He walked towards her, looking straight into her eyes so that if his courage gave out he would be forced to say something. Come over to the burrows, he would say. He would tell her about that place, but the way she raised her head, he suspected she knew it.

SHE RAISED HER head and opened her mouth, her answer already there. She inhabited that place, was already there, her open mouth like it was for the lifeguard when he pressed his hand to her stomach, pushed the salt water out, then put his lips to her lips and blew.

Skin

THE ODD FANTASIES we people our days with; she had just pierced her finger with the knife, and from between the petals of split skin blood was oozing. It was coming in one large drop, growing as it came. Till her detached face reflects in the crimson.

But in fact the knife had missed her forefinger. It had cut round the gritty root of the lopped-off stem and was now splicing the orb into tiny segments. Her eyes were running. Cracked pieces of onion spitting moisture at her, bringing tears, misting her view of the enamel sink. The sink that was, despite the distortion of tears, as solidly present as it had been yesterday.

She was absorbed in the onion's deceit; its double-take. She had peeled layer upon layer from it and was anticipating a centre. Something like a fulcrum, of which she could say: here the skin ends; here the onion begins. And instead there was this endless succession of them, each like a smaller clenched fist, fading eventually into insignificance. Embryonic cell-like tissue which gave the appearance of a core. But in fact the same layers in miniature. Ah, she sighed, almost disappointed, looking at the handful of diced onion on the draining-board. She gathered these in her hands and shook them into the bowl. She washed her hands, to dispel the damp oily feeling, the acid smell. Then she turned her back on the sink, gazed absently on the kitchen table.

She had an apron on her, something like a smock. Flowers bloomed on it, toy elephants cavorted on their hind legs. There was lace round the neck and a bow-tied string at the back and a slit-pocket across the front into which she could place her hands or dry her fingers. Above it her face, which was uneventfully trim, and just a little plain. She was wearing high-heeled house slippers and an over-tight bra. Her shoulder was shifting uncomfortably because of it. When one rests one notices such things. She was resting. From the diced onions, carrots, chunks of meat, whole potatoes on the draining-board. From the black-and-white pepper tins on the shelf above it.

There were two large windows on the sink side of the room. On the wall opposite was a row of small single-paned windows, high up, near the roof. The midday sun came streaming in the large window from behind her. She saw it as a confluence of rays emanating from her. When she shifted, even her shoulder, there would be a rapid rippling of light and shadow on the table cloth. Blue light it was, reflecting the blueness of the kitchen decor. For everything was blue here, the pantry door, the dresser, the walls were painted in rich emulsion, varying from duck-egg to cobalt. And the day was a mild early September, with a sky that retained some of August's scorched vermilion. The image of the Virgin crossed her silent vacant eyes. She had raised her hand to her hair and saw the light break through her fingers. She thought of the statue in the hall; plastic hands with five plastic sunrays affixed to each; streaming towards the feet, the snake, the water-bowl. Mother of Christ.

She had been humming the first phrases of a tune. She stopped it when she returned abruptly to the sink, to the window, to the strip of lard—sparrow meat—hanging outside. She chopped the meat into neat quarters and dumped them with the vegetables into a saucepan. She placed the saucepan on a slow-burning ring. Then she began washing her hands again. The scent of onion still clung to them. Pale hands, made plump by activity, swelling a little round the wrist and round the spot where the tarnished engagement-ring pulled the flesh inwards. She massaged separately the fingers of each hand, rapidly and a little too harshly; as if she were vexed with them, trying to coax something from them. Their lost freshness.

Several inches of water in the sink; a reflection there—two hands caressing, a peering face swimming in the mud-coloured liquid, strewn over with peel. She grabbed hold of the knife and plunged it, wiping it clean with her bare thumb and forefinger. And again came the image—blood oozing, in large crimson drops. But her finger didn't gape. The knife emerged clean.

She pulled the sink plug then, hearing the suck, scouring the residue of grit and onion-skin with her fingers. She dried her hands, walked with the towel into the living-room.

There there was a low-backed modern sofa, two older tattered armchairs and a radiogram piled with magazines. She sat in the sofa, easing herself into its cushioned supports. She fiddled with the radio dial, turned it on, heard one blare of sound and switched it off again. The silence struck her; the chirp of a sparrow outside, clinging to the strip of lard. In another minute she was restless again, leafing through the magazines, flicking impatiently over their pages.

A housewife approaching middle-age. The expected listlessness about the features. The vacuity that suburban dwelling imposes, the same vacuity that most likely inhabited the house next door. But she was an Irish housewife, and as with the whole of Irish suburbia, she held the memory of a half-peasant background fresh and intact. Noticeable in her dealings with the local butcher. She would bargain, oblivious of the demands of propriety. She would talk about childhood with an almost religious awe, remembering the impassioned innocence of her own. And, although house-proud, rigorous tidiness made her impatient; she had a weakness for loose-ends.

And in her the need for the inner secret life still bloomed. It would come to the fore in odd moments. A fragment of a song, hummed for a bar or two, then broken off. A daydream. She would slide into it like a suicide easing himself into an unruffled canal. She would be borne off, swaying, for a few timeless moments. She would hardly notice the return. And for occasional stark flashes, she would be seized by a frightening admixture of religious passion and guilt, bordering on a kind of painful ecstasy; the need, the capacity for religiously intense experience of living; and in consequence of the lack of this, a deep residue of guilt. At times like this she would become conscious of anything red and bloodlike, anything blue or bright, any play of light upon shade.

But if she were asked how she lived, she would have replied: happily. And if she were asked what happiness meant she wouldn't even have attempted an answer.

She found herself rummaging among the magazines searching out one she had been reading yesterday. She recalled a story in it about the habits of Swedish housewives. Certain of them who would drive from their homes between the hours of two and four in the afternoon, out to the country, and there offer themselves to men. The event would take place in a field, under a tree, in a car. And afterwards, they would straighten their clothes, return home to find the timing-clock on the oven at nought, the evening meal prepared. It had disgusted her thoroughly at first glance. But something in it had made her read to the finish. The image, perhaps, of a hidden garden, sculpted secretly out of the afternoon hours, where flowers grew with unimaginable freedom.

Now she was feeling the same compulsion. "Weekend" was the name, she remembered, selecting one from the pile. She opened it at the centre page. A glaring headline there, in vulgar black print: "SWEDISH HOUSEWIVES' AFTERNOON OF SIN." And a picture; a woman standing by a clump of trees, in a shaded country lane. A man in the distance watching her. A parked car.

She closed it instantly. It had disgusted her again. But as she sat there, the sound of distant cars coming to her from the road, her fingers began drumming impatiently on the wooden top of the radio. Something about it drew her. The sun, the glossy green of the foliage. The man's dark predatory back. Not the cheapness, the titillating obscenity. Not that.

Then she was moving towards the front door. Her tweed walking coat was hanging in the alcove. Outside, rows of starlings laced the telegraph-wires. Motionless black spearheads, occasionally breaking into restless wheeling flights, to return again to their rigid formations. The same expectant stasis in her, her drumming fingers, like fluttering wings. She was a starling. The sudden, unconscious burst of disquiet. The animal memory of a home more vibrant, more total than this. The origin-track; the ache for aliveness.

All the way through the hall, out the front door, her fingers drummed. As she turned the ignition-key in the dashboard the engine's purr seemed to echo this drumming.

Howth was facing her as she drove, answering her desperate need for open spaces. Slim spearlike poplars passed her on her left. Oaks gnarled and knotted to bursting-point. Ash and elder, their autumn leaves discoloured by traffic-dust. She drove mechanically. She hardly noticed the line of cars coming towards her. Only the earth to her right, a dull metal plate today. Beyond it, as if thrusting through its horizon with a giant hand, the Hill of Howth.

Her forefinger still tapping on the steering-wheel. Scrubbing vegetables had banished most of the varnish from the nail. Today she didn't notice. A car swerved into her lane and away. She had a moment's vision of herself as a bloodied doll, hanging through a sharded windscreen. She drew a full breath and held it, her lungs like a balloon pressing at her breasts.

She pulled in at a causeway that led across marshlands to the open sea. She quenched the engine and gave herself time to absorb the shock of silence. Then she opened the door, got out, her fingers drumming on the metal roof.

Sounds that could have been the unbending of grass or the scurrying of insects. The lapping hiss of tide from the marshlands, its necklace of canals. But now she was here she wasn't sure why she had come. What to do with "this"—as if the scene before her were some kind of commodity. It was the silence. The sheer pervasiveness of it.

She ran from the car door to the edge of the causeway in an attempt at the abandonment she imagined one should feel. There was a drop there, then mudflats awaiting tide. Nothing came of it, however. Only the sense of her being a standing, awkward thing among grasses that crept, tides that flowed. It didn't occur to her to fall, flatten herself with them, roughen her cheek with the ragwort and sea-grass. She began to walk.

There were ships, tankers most likely, on the rim of the sea. As she walked through the burrows she saw hares bounding. She saw the sun, weak, but still potent. She saw a single lark spiralling towards it. She saw, when she reached it, a restful strand dissolve on either side into an autumn haze. It was empty of people.

The sand rose in flurries with her steps. She had worn the wrong shoes—those high-heeled slippers. Useless, she thought, slipping them off.

The sea amazed her when she reached it. Surging, like boiling green marble. Very high too, from yesterday's spring tide. There was a swell, beginning several yards out, that reached her in ripples. Each wave seemed to rise like a solid thing, laced with white foam, subsiding into paltriness just when she felt it would engulf her. Swelling, foaming, then retreating. The sun glistening coldly off it. She felt spray on her cheek. Wet, ice-cold, the feel of church floors, green altar-rails.

She decided to risk a paddle. She glanced round her and saw nothing but a black dot, like a rummaging dog, in the distance. So she opened her coat, hitched up her skirt, unpeeled her stockings. She'd stay near the edge.

She threw them, with her slippers, to a spot she judged safe from the incoming tide. She walked in, delighted with the tiny surging ripples round her ankles. Her feet were soon blue with the cold. She remembered her circulation and vowed not to stay long. But the freshness of it! The clean salt wetness, up around her calves now! It deserved more than just an ankle-paddle. And soon she was in it up to her knees, with the rim of her skirt all sodden. The green living currents running about her legs, the rivers of puffy white foam surrounding her like a bridal wreath. She hitched up her dress then, the way young girls do, tucking it under their knickers to look like renaissance princes, and felt the cold mad abandon of wind and spray on her legs. A wave bigger than the others surged up wetting her belly and thighs, taking her breath away. The feel of it, fresh and painful, icy and burning! But it was too much, she decided. At her age, skirt tucked up in an empty sea.

She turned to the strand and saw a man there, a wet-tailed cocker-spaniel at his heels, bounding in a flurry of drops. She froze. He had seen her, she was sure of that, though his eyes were now on the dog beside him. The sight of his tan overcoat and his dark oiled hair brought a desolate panic to her. The shame, she thought, glancing wildly about for her stockings and shoes.

But the sea must have touched her core with its irrational ceaseless surging. For what she did then was to turn back, back to the sea, picking high delicate steps through its depths, thinking: He sees me. He sees my legs, my tucked-up skirt, the outlines of my waist clearly through the salt-wet fabric. He is more excited than I am, being a man. And there was this pounding, pounding through her body, saying: this is it. This is what the sea means, what it all must mean. And she stood still, the sea tickling her groin, her eyes fixed on the distant tanker, so far-off that its smokestack seemed a brush stroke on the sky, its shape that of a flat cardboard cut-out. Around it the sea's million dulled glimmering mirrors.

But she was wrong. And when she eventually turned she saw how wrong, for the man was now a retreating outline, like the boat, the dog beside him a flurrying black ball. And she thought, Ah, I was wrong about that too. And she walked towards the shore, heavy with the knowledge of days unpeeling in layers, her skirt and pants sagging with their burden of water.

Her Soul

"I've lost my wife," the man said.
"And I've lost my soul" . . . .
She leaned back on the banisters. The man swayed as he came down, spilling his orange-coloured drink on her dress. But the dress was patterned in broad horizontal stripes like a spinning-top and all of the stripes were some shade of orange so she didn't remark on it. She held on to the banisters swaying, wondering how it had gone so easily.

It hadn't gone the way it should have, like a silver bird flying upwards leaving the shell of her behind, of an aeroplane glinting. It had slipped out of her as if she was a glass and it was the liquid, she filled too full, it slopping down her wet side. And being insubstantial it had disappeared, melted like quick ice, not giving her a chance to grab or shout come back. Well, she thought.

The music came from the room downstairs and the ecstatic party sounds. She flattened the damp side of her heliotrope dress with her hand.

"My soul," she muttered to the grey suit and the loose neck-tie that was ascending the stairs.

"My undying love," he said and she wondered whether this was taunt or invitation. She was past recognition of witticisms. She looked down the stairs seeing the broad swipes of shadow and the broad swipes of light and thought how easily it could have slipped through one of them. Sidled through, sly thing that it was. Her eyes ran with the shadowed stairs, bumped with them down to the stairs-end closet. Coats hung there, etched and still. Broad folds and shadows. That's it, it slipped, she thought, like a shadow slips when the sun goes in. And every shadow and every fold of cloth became an invitation to her, a door behind which the shadow-world lay, through which one could slip and float and be insubstantial and pure, like gas released from a test-tube, not heavy and swaying like in this bright-light world. That's it, she thought.

Suddenly the shadows tottered and wheeled and the cream-white walls swung dark and bright and she thought she would be blessed with entry into that shadow-world where her soul perhaps was. But then she saw the man with the open tie above her on the stairs tapping the light-bulb.

"My soul," she said, thinking it was a party and one must say something.

"My beard and whiskers," he said, tapping the bulb.

"Stop it, will you." She covered her eyes.

"I'm sorry," he said. "Have some."

He held out his hand, proffering a glass. She saw a silver bracelet over the hair on the wrist, then a white cuff and a grey sleeve. At the top of the sleeve was a loose tie and a fattish white neck and brown eyes and a smiling mouth. The eyes were fixed on her left ear and the mouth smiling at something adjacent to it, over her shoulder.

And she fancied, taking the glass, that that was it. Her soul hadn't dripped or flown but had retreated to some point beyond her shoulder; that point towards which people looked, the point posited by his eyes, his eyes that had ripped it from her breast or wherever, from under the heliotrope dress where it should have lain pulsing and whole; had done so because there it was safe, there it was distant.

All the anger at the loss of her soul ran through her so strongly that she imagined she could somehow get it back, that by smashing the glass with her hand on it against the banisters it would somehow appear, reappear with the real pain and the ripped palm and the red sharded pieces of glass.

But she sipped from the glass instead, thinking she would never know, perhaps it's better gone, rolling the whisky about her palate and her tongue, wondering what to say.

Outpatient

WHEN SHE CAME back she was thinner than ever. She had always been thin, but now her thinness seemed to have lost its allure, her mouth seemed extraordinarily wide, all her facial bones prominent. And when he looked at her he stopped thinking of love and began to think of necessary companionship, mature relationship and things like that. It will be better, he told her, when we get the house. And he put his arms around her on the steps and knew that he had married her for that peculiar quality of thinness that had been fashionable that year. Somewhere inside him he felt obscurely angry at her for having let her stock of beauty fade; for standing before him in the same tweed cloak in which she had left, like a thin pear topped by flat brown hair and brown eyes, an oval of skin the colour of thawed snow. He felt cheated. He also felt virtuous, accepting as he was her flawed self, and only a little ashamed. And all the while she felt his arms around her on the steps she had left and imagined the house to be rectangular, as all houses are, with rectangular rooms and a pebble-dash front. And a garden. There would have to be a garden.

They walked up the steps and up the stairs, past the many flats into their own. She heard the old woman moving round above them. She hasn't died yet, she asked him. No, he whispered, and looked shocked. He told her there was nothing to be ashamed of, that it wasn't as if she had had a breakdown, just that she needed a rest. He asked her what it was like, said that her letters hadn't told him much. She told him that she had seen the Burren and described the burnt mountain landscapes. She told him about St Brigit's Well and described the long line of pilgrims stretching up the mountain and the faded holy pictures

inside the grotto and the four crutches of the cripples who had
been miraculously cured. Do you believe it, she asked him. Do
you believe they were cured? Perhaps, he said, they were never
really crippled, or the cure was psychosomatic. But miraculously, she asked, not miraculously? and the word sounded like
a peal of trumpets in her ears, she saw the biblical walls tumbling. And he didn't answer, he looked at her quickly once, and
then took her by both shoulders and stood back from her, as if
complimenting her on something. It did you good, he said, and
it will be better this time. Won't it?

She heard the old woman moving again and pictured her
wrinkled thin head bending over the one-bar electric fire. He had
let his hands drop. They were standing facing one another,
neither looking. Mentally she took several steps backwards. She
saw two people in a room with three white walls and one orange
wall, with blue-coloured armchairs, prints of old Dublin and
poster reproductions. There was a hum of traffic through the
window from way below. If she had seen it as an extract from
a film she would have known it to be the last-but-one scene of
some domestic tragedy. And she knew it wasn't going to work
once more, she could see the end from the extract, but it
wouldn't fail tragically, it would piffle out, with barely a whisper. For she knew that once she could look at herself as if she
were another person it would not work, there would be no real
pain even. And she discovered to her surprise that she thirsted
for pain and reality. What was it about this house, she asked. It's
a bargain, he began . . .

He watched her undress as if wondering would her thinness
be the same underneath. It was, except that her belly now
seemed to sag outwards. She was wearing the tight girlish underwear that always had excited him. He looked at her face as little
as possible so as to remain aroused, concentrating on her thin
buttocks and stark ribs. He had determined not to sleep, he had
determined this should stay even if the rest failed. He decided
that her sagging belly was due to her stance. He looked in her

face and saw her eyes, unbearably brown and her flat hair. Come, he said.

She was amazed he wanted it. She was gratified in an automatic romantic manner till she gauged his methodic sensuality and knew he was already thinking of children. She determined to disappoint him and lay flat and rigid. She knew he was disappointed but felt the dome of a great heavy bell around her, she looking out through it, at him lying flat and white, staring at the ceiling. Help me, he said. Promise me you'll help me. I can't, she said, if you don't help me. What does that mean, he asked. It means there's a space between you and me that no-one can help. No-one, he said. She didn't answer. She was composing an equation, of the sum of her need and the sum of his, of the compound of their ability to give and of the small persistent almighty minus in between. Then she pulled herself from between the covers and went out to wash. We'll go to see the house tomorrow, she heard him say and she noticed how the wretchedness of his voice a moment ago had gone. It sounded common-sense and confident, coming to her in the dark of the bathroom.

He mumbled something and turned on his side, with his back to her, when she returned to the bed. He was well into sleep. But she lay awake staring at the wastes of the ceiling, thinking, I've just come back from a place where people walk three miles to see the miraculous crutches and the rotting mass-cards and he—. Her thought stopped here, blocked by something deadening, momentous, stolid. And he what, she thought. She couldn't praise or blame or hate. She thought instead of the equation again, of the sum of his giving and the sum of hers, of their mutual spaces and the ridiculous pathetic minus round which the worlds hinged. She thought herself, rocked herself to sleep, praying for more, for the miraculous plus. She dreamed of meat. She dreamt she was love-making, rigid against his rapid orgasm and above them was hanging a butcher's half-carcass, swinging between ceiling and floor. Gigot or loin, she wondered. Each rib was curved like a delicate half-bow, white, made stark by the red

meat between. She wanted to shake him, and cry out: Look at
that dead meat. But it swung above her, silencing her, glowing,
incandescent.

The next day he drove her to the house, positively angry now
at her silences, more and more repulsed by her battered thinness.
It was in a North-side suburb near Portmarnock beach. Streets
rose up a hill, breezes came from the unseen sea, the salt air was
belied by the system-built houses. They drove up to it and
parked on the opposite side. Its facade, she saw, was a large
rectangle, half red-brick, half pebble dash. What do you think,
he asked. She nodded her head. You'll get nothing better under
eight thou, he said. She didn't answer. She suddenly hated him
for that abbreviated word. She looked at the house, itself like an
abbreviated word, its shape, its texture. Why is it square, she
said, why not round? I want to live in a round house, with a roof
like a cone, with a roof like a witch's hat. She laughed and heard
her laugh echoing strangely in the car. She saw his hands clasp-
ing and unclasping, each finger in its curve on the plastic wheel.
She stopped the laugh quickly then. But the silence rang with the
stopped laugh.

They walked through it and she saw her imagination verified.
They walked through the hall, with its regular stairs rising
upwards, into the kitchen, which gleamed bright steel. They
walked out of the kitchen and up the stairs, through each bedroom and then returned to the kitchen again. What do you
think, he asked. She had her back turned to him and she felt the
great bell descend on her, its brass tongue falling with a threat
she only dreamed of. She turned to his voice, which was tiny and
distant, and saw his horror of silence in his set face. She saw her
face reflected in his pupil, with enlarged thin cheekbones and a
too-wide mouth. Then she longed for the tongue to clang with
its trumpetlike peal as she heard him say: We'll look at the
garden.

And she saw him open the kitchen door, totally without her
fear. She saw through the door the green mound of Howth

Head, a long stretch of sea and a thin elongated smokestack of grey cloud. She saw his square back moving towards the backdrop of waste sea and cloud. He was moving to the paltry green rim of hedge at the end, avoiding the mounds of cement-coloured earth, scraping with the toe of his shoe at the resilient ground. When he reached it he turned. And she walked towards him down the calloused garden wanting to tell him that this house had nothing to do with miracles and trumpets, knowing she would not. There was a wind blowing from the sea, ruffling the hedge, his hair and her kilted skirt.

Tree

THERE WERE two things he could not do, one was drive a car, the other was step out of a car. So she was driving when she saw the tree, she had been driving all week. He was telling her another point of interest about the crumbling landscape round them, the landscape with more points of historical interest per square mile than—something about a woman who was to have a baby at midnight, but who sat on a rock and kept the baby back till dawn, an auspicious hour, and the rock ever after had a dent in it and was called Brigid's—

She saw the tree from about a mile off, since the road they were driving was very straight, rising slowly all the time, with low slate walls that allowed a perfect, rising view. It was late summer and the tree looked like a whitethorn tree and she forgot about local history and remembered suddenly and clearly holidays she had taken as a child, the old Ford Coupe driving down the country lanes and the flowering whitethorn dotting the hedges. It would appear in regular bursts, between yards of dull green. It would be a rich, surprised cream colour, it would remind her of a fist opened suddenly, the fingers splayed heavenwards. It would delight her unutterably and her head would jerk forwards and backwards as each whitethorn passed.

Then something struck her and she stopped the car suddenly. She jerked forward and she heard his head striking the windscreen.

"What's—" he began, then he felt his head. She had interrupted him.

"I'm sorry," she said, "but look at that tree."

"There are no trees." His fingers had searched his forehead

and found a bump. He would be annoyed. "This is a limestone landscape."

She pointed with her finger. His eyes followed her finger and the edges of his eyelids creased as he stared.

"Well, there is a tree, then."

"It's a whitethorn tree," she said. "It's flowering."

"That's impossible," he said. She agreed.

The thought that it was impossible made her warm, with a childish warm delight. She felt the hairs rising on her legs. She felt the muscles in her legs glow, stiff from the accelerator. The impossible possible, she thought. She knew the phrase meant nothing. She remembered an opera where a walking-stick grew flowers. She thought of death, which makes anything possible. She looked at his long Teutonic face, such perfection of feature that it seemed a little deformed.

"But it's white, isn't it."

"Then," he said, "it couldn't be a whitethorn."

"But it's white."

"It's the end of August."

She turned the key in the ignition and drove again. She thought of his slight, perfect body beside her in bed, of its recurrent attraction for her. She thought of his hatred of loud sounds, his habit of standing in the background, the shadows, yet seeming to come forward. She thought of how his weaknesses became his strengths, with a cunning that was perhaps native to his weakness. She thought of all the times they had talked it out, every conceivable mutation in their relationship, able and disable, every possible emotional variant, contempt to fear, since it's only by talking of such things that they are rendered harmless. She drove the car slowly, on the slight upward hill, the several yards to the pub they had arranged to stop at.

"It is possible."

"What is."

"Everything's possible."

He asked would they go in, then.

She opened her door and walked around the car and opened his door. She waited till he had lifted his good leg clear of the car, then held his arm while he balanced himself and lifted out the stiff leg.

She watched him walk across the road and marvelled again at how the stiffness gave him, if anything, a kind of brittle elegance. She saw him reach the pub door, go inside without looking back. Then she looked up the road, curving upwards and the tree off from the road, in the distance. It was still white. Unutterably white.

The pub was black after the light outside. He was sitting by the long bar, drinking a glass of beer. Beside him was another glass, and a bottle of tonic-water. Behind the bar was a woman with a dark western face, ruined by a pair of steel glasses. She was talking, obviously in answer to a question of his.

"Cornelius O'Brien lived in the lower one," she said. "Owned more than them all put together. A great packer."

"Packer?"

"Jury-packer," she said, as if it was a term of office.

He leant forward, his face eager with another question. She slipped into the seat beside him. She poured the tonic-water into the glass, wondering why it was he always bought her that. She must have expressed a preference for it once, but she couldn't remember when. Once she drank whiskey, she remembered, and now she drank tonic. And sometime in between she had changed.

"Why did you get me this," she interrupted.

He looked up, surprised. Then smiled, a fluid smile.

"Because you always drink it."

"Once I drank whiskey."

The wrinkles formed in clusters round his eyes.

"I remember. Yes. Why did you stop?"

She drank it quietly, trying to remember, listening to his further question about the crumbling castles. The woman answered, speaking the way children do, using words they don't understand. She used phrases to describe the dead inhabitants of those castles that were like litanies, that had filtered through years to her, that must have once had meaning. She was cleaning a glass and her eyes looked vacant as her mouth spoke the forgotten phrases.

She stared at the ice in her tonic-water. She watched it melt, slowly. She wondered about phrases, how they either retain the ghost of a meaning they once had, or grope towards a meaning they might have. Then she suddenly, vitally, remembered the taste of whiskey. Gold, and volatile, filling not the tongue but the whole mouth.

"Whitethorn," she said, loud, out of the blue, as if it were a statement.

The woman stopped cleaning the glass and looked at her. He put his hand round his glass and looked at her.

"Have you come far, then," the woman asked.

He mentioned a town a hundred miles east.

"A long way, all right," the woman said. Then she glanced from him to her.

"Is it herself who drives?"

She saw his hand tighten round the glass. She remembered the taste of whiskey. She said:

"He has a bad leg. There are two things he can't do. Get out of a car, and drive a car. But otherwise everything's fine. Isn't that right, John?"

He had already gone towards the door. She fumbled in her pocket to find fifty pence. She couldn't and so she left a pound.

He was standing by the door of the car.

"Why did you have to jabber on like that?"

"Why did you order me a tonic?"

"You're impossible."

"Nothing's impossible."

"Get in."

She drove. He swore at her in considered, obscene phrases as she drove. She knew he would swear like that, slowly and sadistically, scraping every crevice of her womanhood, till his anger had died down. So she drove with her eyes on the blaze far up the road, like a surprised fist with its fingers towards the sky, the brilliant cream-white of a dice-cube. As she drove nearer it seemed to swim in front of her eyes, to expand, to explode, and yet still retain its compact white. She could hear their breathing as she drove, hers fast like an animal that is running, his slow, like an animal that must stand in the one place. Then the white seemed to fill her vision and she stopped. She looked at the trunk below the white and the long field between it and the road. Then she looked at him.

He was crying, and his face looked more beautiful than ever through the tears.

"I love you," he said.

"I'm leaving," she said.

"Again?" he asked.

He grabbed her, half angry, half afraid, but she had the door open already and she slipped away. She walked round the car and looked at him.

"I don't—" she began, but her words were drowned by the sudden blast of the horn. His hand was on it, his knuckles white, his body was bent forward as if all his strength was needed to keep the horn pressed. She could hear the awful blare in her ears and could see his lips moving, saying something. She shouted at him to take his hand off and his lips moved again, saying the same something, the same three words. She made out the three words then and turned from his face and ran.

She ran to the slate wall and clambered over it, scraping her shins. She felt the grass under her feet and put her hands over her ears. She was shocked by the sudden silence, like a sudden immersion in water. She was walking, but it was as if through a mental landscape, no sound but the strange humming of her eardrums. She felt she had closed her eyes and found this field, not driven to it. She knew her feet were walking her towards the tree, but it was as if the tree was coming towards her. The landscape rising with each step and each step bringing the land-scape nearer. The tree on the hill, with its white made manage-able now, small, tangible, familiar. She counted her steps like a little girl does and each step misplaced her hands and rang in her ears. Then something struck her about the tree, not really white, more an off-grey colour. She took three more steps and it came nearer, with the hill behind it, and its blossoms seemed to flap. But blossoms don't flap, she thought, they are still and pristine, they burst or moult, not flap and she must have run then for it came nearer in several large leaps.

And it was there then, bare rough whitethorn with scores of tiny rags tied to each branch, pieces of handkerchief, shirttails, underwear, shift, masquerading as blossom. She thought of peo-ple wishing, tying these proxy blossoms. She thought of her and her hope that it had blossomed and them, making it blossom with their hope. She wondered again what hope meant, what impossible meant, but there was less scope to her wondering. She saw faded holy pictures nailed to the bottom of the trunk but couldn't read the pleas written on them. She took her hands from her ears to tear one off and the wail of the horn flooded her again, distant, plaintive, pleading. She tore a picture off, parts of it crumbled in her fingers, but she read "To Brigid for favours granted, August 1949." And the horn wailed like pain.

A Love

THERE WERE no cars in Dublin when I met you again, the streets had been cleared for the funeral of the President who had died. I remembered you talking about him and I thought of how we would have two different memories of him. He was your father's generation, the best and the worst, you said. I remembered your father's civil war pistol, black and very real, a cowboy gun. It was that that first attracted me, me a boy beyond the fascination of pistols but capable of being seduced by a real gun owned by a lady with real bullets—I shattered two panes in your glasshouse and the bullet stuck in the fence beyond the glasshouse shaking it so it seemed to be about to fall into the sea and float with the tide to Bray Head. Then you took the gun from me saying no-one should play with guns, men or boys and put the hand that held it in your blouse, under your breast. And I looked at you, an Irish woman whose blouse folded over and was black and elegant in the middle of the day, whose blouse hid a gun besides everything else. But except that you smiled at me with a smile that meant more than all those I would just have been a kid bringing a message from his father to a loose woman. As it was you walked over the broken glass away from me and I stepped after you over the broken pieces to where the view of the sea was and you began to teach me love.

And when we met again there were no cars and the headlines talked about love and guns and the man who had died and I wondered how different your memory of him would be from mine. It was a stupid pursuit since I had no memory of him other than from photographs and then only a big nose and bulging eyes and spectacles but I knew you would be changed and I knew I was changed and I wanted to stop thinking about it.

70

There were no cars but there were flowers in the giant pots on O'Connell Bridge, there was a band somewhere playing slow music and there were crowds everywhere on the pavement, women mostly who remembered him as something important, women who clutched handbags to their stomachs and stared at the road where the funeral would soon pass. I could sense the air of waiting from them, they had all their lives waited, for a funeral, a husband, a child coming home, women your age, with your figure, they had loved abstractly whereas you had loved concretely with a child like me. That was the difference I told myself but it was probably only that I knew you and I didn't know them. But that had always been the difference, all women had been a mother to someone but you had been a lover to me. And I focused my eyes on the empty street with them and wondered had that difference faded.

I WENT INTO the cafe then and it smelt of Dublin, Ireland, the musty femininity of the women waiting on the kerb for the men to pass, dead, heroic, old and virginal. I sat by the plate-glass window and looked at the shiny chrome espresso machine, a cloud of steam rising from it. A girl in a blue smock with an exhausted face brought me coffee and I felt for the first time that I was back somewhere. I tasted the coffee and got the cheap caffeine bite, details like that, the girl's legs, too thin so the nylons hung in folds around them. Outside I could hear the brass band coming nearer, louder like the slowed step soldiers use in funerals. I knew I was out of step, it was all militarism now, like air in a blister, under the skin, it was swelling, the militarism I had just learned of before, in the school textbooks. Then I remembered something else about him, the man who had died, he had been the centre of the school textbooks, his angular face and his thirties collar and his fist raised in a gesture of defiance towards something out there, beyond the rim of the brown photograph, never defined. And I wondered whether I'd rather be out of step here or in step in London, where the passions are rational. And I felt the nostalgia of the emigrant, but it was as if I was still away, as if here in the middle of it all I was still distant, remembering, apart from it. I shook myself but couldn't get rid of the feeling. Something had happened to me since leaving, something had happened to me long before I left, but then everything changes, I told myself, and some things die. So I just looked out the plate-glass window and listened to the slow brass, swelling more all the time.

Then I saw someone looking like you coming down the street towards the cafe and as that someone came nearer I saw it was you, still you, your hair had got a little greyer but still kept that luxuriant brownness, your face had got thinner and fatter, thinner round the cheekbones, fatter round the jaw and neck. You hadn't seen me yet but I couldn't get myself to rise out of the seat so you would see me, I wanted to look at you like you were a photograph. I was remembering that letter of my father's, the only letter, that said you were sick and you did look sick, in the quiet way of bad sicknesses, cancer and the like. And then you opened the glass door and the brass music grew to an orchestra and the door closed and the music faded again and still I couldn't get up. And you were standing over me.

"NEIL!" you said.

"Yes," I said.

"Well," you said.

"Yes," I said again.

And then you sat down beside me, I was a child who isn't saying something, the thin girl came over to take your order. We were the only two in the cafe, you were talking, I was listening to you, quite natural, ordinary things after all. We were different, I was a young adult, you were an old adult, we both fingered coffee cups, mine cold, yours hot. I tried obscurely to remember, I had been an Irish boy with greased hair and a collarless leather jacket, you had been a single woman who kept a guesthouse in a town called Greystones and now both of us were neither, my hair was dry and short, it came straight down my forehead and

my forehead had a few lines, though people still told me sometimes that I looked sixteen, you were living in a house somewhere on the South Side, you didn't work now though the car
keys you squeezed in your palm and the fur sleeves that hung
dead from your wrists made you look well-off, in an extrava-
gant, haphazard way.

Then you mentioned the dead man outside.

AND SOMEHOW it began to come right. I noticed the black silk
blouse under the coat, the loose and mottled skin where your
neck met your breast. I remembered the nights lying in your old
creaking bed that looked out on the sea, our movements like a
great secret between us, silent, shocking movements, our silence
a guard against my father who had the room down below, our
lovemaking a quiet desecration of the holiday town, of the
church at the top of the hill, of the couples you fed so properly
at mealtimes, of my embarrassed adolescence, the guilt you tried
to banish in me, the country, the place, the thing you tried to hit
at through me you taught me to hit through you. And all the
time for me there was my father lying underneath, cold most
likely, and awake and I wanted him to hear the beast I was
creating with you, I wanted him to hear it scratching, creaking
through to him from above, for your body was like the woman
he must have loved to have me, I had seen her in those brown
faded photographs with a floppy hat and a cane, in a garden, like
you but fatter, with a lot of clothes that came off, the coloured
dresses and blouses first, then the white underclothes, dampened
under the armpits, between the legs. And when you undressed
on the beach and I watched you from the road, watched each
thing falling in a bundle on the sand, you could have been her,
you could have been anyone's mother only you were naked with
a belly that drooped a little and a triangle of hair underneath it.
Only that when you saw me you didn't shy from my frightened
stare, you smiled. That smile began it. But what perpetuated it
was something outside, my mathematical father lying sleepless

on his bed, your civil-war gun, rosaries, that rain-soaked politician with his fist raised, clenched. Against something. Something.

THE BRASS BAND seemed much nearer now, going ahead of the same politician's cortege, ceremonial, thudding slow brass. I was watching you drinking your coffee. The brass music was cascading about you. I looked at the thin part of your face, you had no makeup on, your eyes looked almost ordinary. You were different and the same, I was different and the same, I knew that that is how things happen. And yet I'd met you because I wanted something more. We are all different threads, I told myself and once we had woven each other's threads into something like a bow. Once.

"WELL."
   We were stuck on that word. Then I plunged.
   "What are we going to do then, before I go back?"
   "Back where?"
   And I don't know whether you wanted to know, but I told you it all, about the hairdresser's in Kensal Rise, the women who tipped me pound notes if I touched their plump shoulders and told them they were too young for a blue rinse.
   "Is that what you do."
   "Yes."
   And I told you about the cockney queen I shared a room with who I despised but who could be warm when—
   "And don't you act now—"
   And yes, I told you about the sweaty revues, revue being synonymous with theatrical sex, I told you about the empty stages where we rehearsed in our underwear and fingered each other's goose pimples, simulated copulation. Then I stopped, because you were drinking your coffee again and your unmadeup face looked sad, like an adolescent, the one I had been. And for a moment I was the experienced one, I clutched the gun, under my breasts, between the sheaves of my black blouse.

"We'll go to Clare. Lisdoonvarna."

"Why there," I asked.

"I am past my prime. They are places for people past their prime."

And I wondered should you say "prime" or "primes," I thought of all the hotels and guesthouses I had never been to. I knew middle-aged people went to those places and met men and took the waters and married maybe and drank sherries looking at the Atlantic, in bars that were probably closed now for De Valera's death.

"It's Autumn and everyone there will be past their prime. I want to see the bachelors court the spinsters. I want to take the waters. I want to drive in a Morris Minor past the Burren and look at the unusual flowers."

There was an accusation in your voice as if you were trying to tell me something, something I didn't want to hear. I thought maybe you wanted to fit yourself, label yourself and I wondered would your conformity be as bizarre as my attempts at it had been.

You talked about happiness then, a murderous happiness that followed you round like a pet dog. And I looked at you, you had pressed your unpainted lips together, the blood had gone out of them and I saw the need for happiness that had ravaged you, I wondered what deity it was that would label you old maid or spinster when you had once pressed that happiness on me. Then I heard the band outside, so loud now, and the cortege was passing and the band was playing the old nationalist tunes to a slow tempo. I felt I was watching an animal dying through the plate-glass window, an animal that was huge, murderous, contradictory and I looked up at your face, not much older really than when I had last seen you and I looked out the plate-glass window again at the funeral of the man I didn't remember, the man you would have remembered. I wondered what your memories were, your associations. And I looked at your eyes, bare and washed clean and I somehow knew.

WE WALKED outside then and the brass music became a deafening thud. We walked slowly down the street, we couldn't talk, the music was so loud. I bought a newspaper at the corner of Abbey Street and saw a headline about the funeral that was crawling along beside us. We passed a TV sales shop where a crowd of people were staring at a white screen, staring at the death being celebrated behind them.

AS I REMEMBER you I define you, I choose bits of you and like a child with a colouring-book, I fill you out. The car-keys are swinging on your finger, your forefinger and thumb choose one, insert it in the lock and your whole hand tenses in the turning. Your car is like you said, a Morris Minor. It's grey and covered in dents and the chrome is rusty. Your hand turning is reddish, sunburnt, which accentuates more its many creases. Then a man-sized watch and the sleeve of your coat where the fur has rubbed off.

Once it was desire I filled you out with, not memory. You were a blown-up photograph to me, a still from a film. I brought the youthful sullenness I learnt from the hit songs to you. I ate chips before I came to you, my fingers stank of vinegar, my breath of nicotine. And you played with me, you let me fill you out, you played Ava Gardner to my James Dean. But I chose, I was arbitrary, I took what I wanted. Your brown hair, your anxious mouth, your bare feet—on the straw bedroom mat. I took some and left the rest, I didn't know what the rest meant, I didn't know what varicose veins meant or fallen arches or lace curtains, respectability, spinsterhood. I plead guilty but ignorant, I didn't know what woman meant.

"CAN YOU DRIVE?"

I said no. I said I would like to, I would like to feel machinistic and free but my father never drove so no-one taught me.

"What do you mean," you asked. "Machinistic—"

And I hadn't known what I meant, I got confused, I said something about the wheel driving, following the white line. Then you were quiet for a while, whether from tactfulness or not I don't know and then—

"I wasn't made for cars."

I didn't believe you, you had shaped this car to fit you. You drove it like it fitted you, through the city that was empty, that had put its best side out for the man who had died. The streets were clean, the buildings were respectful, they seemed to curtsy before us as you drove. Then they got thinner and thinner and we were on the dual carriageway, driving west.

"I IDOLISED him once."

I meant to ask you about your sickness but the words wouldn't come. So you talked while you drove, abstracted talk.

"I was taught to idolise him, everyone was. I remember standing at meetings, holding my father's hand, waving a tricolour, shouting Up Dev. My father wore a cloth cap and a trenchcoat, everyone did then."

Your eyes were squinted towards the road as if you saw what you were remembering on it.

"His face was like a schoolteacher's. Or maybe all schoolteachers tried to look like him. You could never see his eyes clearly because of his glasses. They were the first thing you noticed after his nose."

We were passing Monasterevin. The town looped in a semicircle round your car.

"Have you ever been to the West?"

"No," I said.

"You'll never understand this country till you have."

Your voice sounded older, consciously older, something valedictory in it that made me remember the night my father took you out and me with him as his fifteen-years-old son, mature enough for adult company, my father being a lecturer in maths and a widower, a natural partner for you who was single, who kept the guesthouse he stayed in. We went to a variety in Bray where a Scottish comedian told Irish jokes and a youth with a guitar sang Lonnie Donegan songs and two girls with a ukelele sang George Formby and kicked their legs on either side of the stand-up mike. And afterwards we went for a meal in the Royal Hotel, we ate roast beef and drank sherry. I poured your sherry with the distance he had trained me in and I sat at the far end of the table while you both talked, he at length, you with many pregnant pauses. You talked about life, about friends in public life, who you knew of through your father, who he knew of through his work, he prided himself on both his aloofness from the world and his reserved contact with it. You were beautiful and intimidating in a navy dress and shawl and while in your silences you spoke to me, me in my greased hair and the suit I was told to wear, in your conversation you spoke to him and you managed the pretending so adroitly that in the end I was fooled and I screamed at you afterwards and it took three days for our mutual secret to build up again between us, for me to hold the you I wanted in my unwashed arms, selfishly and viciously, for you to tell me again about love and irreligion, about other countries where women are young at the age of thirty-nine and boys are men at fifteen.

"ARE YOU HAPPY?"

"Sometimes," I said.

"You used to be. You used to be very quiet, very joyful and very sullen."

We were passing Portlaoise, the barbed-wire towers of the prison and the red wall of the mental hospital.

"It was all in your face," you said. "In the way your snub-nose twitched—"

And we both laughed then, it sounded stupid but we laughed and your laugh was like a peal, you could have been standing in the broken pieces of glass again, beside the glasshouse, laughing. I tightened my nose like a rabbit the way I used to do, then I flushed in embarrassment doing it and that made you laugh louder, so loud that you began coughing and had to stop the car and wipe your mouth. There was blood on the Kleenex you wiped it with.

"We're different," you said.

"Yes," I said. And you looked at me and giggled again. Like someone very young. Too young. You put your arms around me and kissed my face and I stayed very quiet, feeling you again, smelling you again. Your lips opened on my cheek and I could hear a tiny whistle off your breath.

"Aren't we?"

"Yes," I said. "We're different," and I kissed you back so you could feel how different. But you stopped me.

"Don't try and change me."

"How could I?"

"You could," you said. "You could change me back."

BUT YOU WERE happy then, weren't you? You began to drive faster, swerving gaily to avoid pigeons. You asked me about myself and my father and I answered both as well as I could. You still coughed every now and then and once you had to stop the car, your whole body tensed as if you were in pain. Your fingers clenched the wheel, they seemed to get even thinner and the bones on the backs of your hands were thin, leading like a scallop to the fingers. But you got over it then, you began to drive, you told me not to mind you, that you were only dying, it's a common complaint and you laughed like before and I laughed with you. Then we stopped in a pub for a drink and I drank a gin while you drank a pint of stout and the barman remarked on how it's normally the other way round.

WHEN WE WERE driving again we saw a fat girl standing by a petrol-pump following every car that passed her with her eyes and thumb. You wanted to stop but I didn't let you, I thought she'd come between us and the laughing. So we drove on and I had a clear view of the disappointment in her large blue eyes as she fumbled with her handbag, realising the car wasn't going to stop after all. And I felt sorry for a moment but your mad peculiar gaiety filled the car again and stopped me feeling sorry.

WHEN WE CAME to Limerick you got quieter and I thought we were stopping since it was almost dark. But you said that you hated it there and you drove on till we came to a sign saying Lahinch and a street that was flanked by burrows and summer houses. You stopped. It was fully dark. We were on the street of a seaside town. I could see a beach at the end of the street, then sea, a different sea from the one we had left. But then all seas are the same, I thought and when we walked down to the beach and watched the tide sucking off the long strand I saw it was the same, like the one that had washed your guesthouse.

I BEGAN TO FEEL it all again, the seaside town, you beside me, wild and intractable and almost old, the bed and breakfast signs, the guesthouses. In the bars men stared at us, men that looked like weekend golfers but I didn't mind, you drank your Guinness while I drank my gin, you talked about happiness so much that I had to tell you to stop.

And then we went to a guesthouse and it was like yours, it had a grey granite front weeping from the sea-breeze, like yours except that it was a man that signed us in, held out the guest book for us with large, country hands. You paid.

I WENT BEHIND you up the stairs. Your breathing was so heavy that it sang in my ears. And then we were in the room and it was so bare, there were two beds, a wash-hand basin, a Virgin and a cinema poster, so seductively bare. You asked me to turn while you undressed. My face must have shown my surprise because before I could answer you turned. And I watched you, I saw your clothes form a little heap around your feet, I saw your shoulders that were very thin and your waist that was almost fat now and your buttocks and your legs. And your skin told me you were definitely older. When you were in your nightgown you turned.

"Come on," you said.

There was a knowledge burning through both of us, it was like the yearning that had been there years before, a secret, like blood. But it wasn't a yearning, it was a question and an answer. You knew that with every garment you took off you were stepping into a past self, a self that had that yearning and you could see from my face that I knew too.

"Come on," you said again.

And I took off my clothes and I wore the nakedness I had worn for you, I was a boy then, and I took off your nightdress so you could wear it too.

I didn't look at you, I put my arms around you, standing there, both of us were breathing, our chests touching. You stepped backwards towards the bed.

"Come on," you said.

AND WE WERE on the bed, the sea was breathing outside like a woman, we were moving together but I wasn't thinking of you, not you now anyway, I was thinking of you before, of the time he brought you out, the second time, the time after which something finished for me and for you and for him too maybe. He brought you to the Great Northern Hotel this time, and me, there were meal-tables there and a small space for dancing to a small three-piece band. And the meal was like before, you laughing with him and being silent every now and then and me pouring sherry for both of you, in good suit and greased hair. And when the meal was finished the reddish lights came on and the dancing began. The band played waltzes and both of you moved across the floor among other shapeless couples, you beautiful, him tall and supremely confident of something as he waltzed. And I sat there looking and saw him for the first time not as my father who wrote equations on sheets of paper into the night and knew a lot about things like sea-shells but as someone young and agile who had the same yearning for you as I had. And as I drank the sherry that you both had left I began to cry, I felt older than him, insanely older, I had the knowledge of you that made him dance so gracefully, that made that difference in him. Then I drank more sherry and saw his hands around your waist almost touching at the back and I knew people do that when they waltz but I began to hate him as I would hate someone my age. Then again I saw his eyes, distant and kind of hopeful, more hopeful than whenever he had looked at me and as I knew the yearning that was behind them I stopped my hate and felt baffled, sad, older than I could bear. The band was playing the "Tennessee Waltz" I remembered and I tried to catch your eye but you were looking the other way, looking strict, virginal, leonine. And then I felt the huge resentment, I couldn't do anything with it, my hands were shaking and I knew something was going to end. And you both came back and I pushed the bottle onto the floor with my hand so it would break, so nobody would know how much I had drunk, hoping it would look like an accident. But the crash was loud and everyone stared and he, my father, lost what he had had with you and went white, and shouted at me and you looked quickly at me and I felt I was a child, being chastened publicly. And later I lay in your bed with this huge resentment and hate. You were asleep when I heard him coming up the first-floor landing and opening the toilet door. And I got up and you were still asleep, I took the gun from your drawer and went down and stood outside the toilet door. And when I heard the chain pull and I knew he was standing buttoning his fly I raised your civil-war gun and fired quickly four times into the door. And there were four bangs and four rapid thuds and I saw each shot wedging, hardly piercing the mahogany. And I ran upstairs knowing something had finished and I gave you the gun and cursed you quietly because it didn't work—

And then I stopped remembering, you were underneath me, I had come inside you in the room in Clare. Your arms were

around my neck, hard, rigid and you said what I was remembering, "It's finished," you said. And you kissed me tenderly and I kissed you back so you could feel how different we were. And I got from your bed quietly, you were exhausted, turning to sleep already. I lay in my own bed listening to the sea outside me, listening to your breathing. There was a luminous statue of the Virgin over you on the wall and a cinema poster. It said I WAS HAPPY HERE in bold letters and showed a woman in a romantic pose looming over a matchbox version of the town we were in. Then I looked at you and saw the eiderdown rising each time you breathed and your body clenching itself every now and then as if you were dreaming of pain. And I knew it had ended but I still thought to myself, maybe tomorrow—

AND TOMORROW you got up and drove, you drove to the town you had told me about, where the bachelors and the spinsters come, where you take the waters. We passed the fat girl again on the road but you didn't stop. And the town was like any other holiday town only more so, with its square of hotels and its peeling wooden verandas and old-fashioned cane chairs lining the verandas.

WE STOPPED in the square. It looked strange to me, a holiday town that's inland. I said this to you, why no sea, and you said, "There's the sulphur waters."

WE WALKED up the street a little. A man stared. I bought a guide-book in a shop. I thought of water and holidays, why they go together. Every building seemed to imply a beach, but there was none. It was as if the sea had once been here, but retreated back to Miltown Malbay, leaving a fossil. Somewhere a front door banged.

IT WAS SAYING something to us, you were saying something, saying, This is it, is me, always has been, the part of me you never saw, didn't want to see. And I believed it then, I knew you

had always been coupled in my mind with hotels, with cane-chairs and ball-and-claw armchairs. And I crossed the square and bought a paper and read more about the President who had died, but in small print now.

WE DROVE OUT to the Spa, to a building that looked like a Swiss hotel, but with a river that seemed to come from underneath it. You asked me did I want to come in and I said no, so you went through the two glass doors alone. I sat in the car wondering whether you drank the waters or bathed in them. A couple passed, wearing suits that must have been too hot for the weather. I shouted at them, "Do you drink the water," I shouted, "or swim in it." The man looked at me and threw his hands up uncomprehendingly. I watched them going through the glass doors and imagined a room with a clean tiled floor through which flowed brackish, slow water. I imagined you taking your clothes off with a lot of older men and women and I watched from the side as you dipped yourself into the spa waters among people who had the minor complaints of middle-age to wash off, who had made the act of faith in water. But then, I might have been quite wrong, maybe you sat on a wooden bench in a line with other people and drank the brack-ish water from a tap.

AND I KNEW it was definitely ending anyhow and that I should forget for your sake the peculiar yearning that sprang in me when my cock sprang to attention in my tight trousers that day you put the gun between your breasts into your blouse. You called it love, I remember. And it must have been.

The
Dream of
a Beast

Kill not the moth nor butterfly
For the Last Judgement draweth nigh.

—WILLIAM BLAKE

1

WHEN I CAME to notice it, it must have been going on for some time. I remember many things about that realisation. Small hints in the organisation of the earth and air, the city. Everyone was noticing things, remarking on things around them, but for me it was critical. Change and decay seemed to be the condition. It wasn't always like that, people would say while waiting for the white bus or circumventing the mounds of refuse that littered the pavements, but from the tone of their voices it seemed just a topic of conversation; the way once they talked about the weather, now they talked about how "things" got worse. It was during a summer that it all quickened. There was the heat, first, that came in the beginning and then stayed. Then fools who for as long as I had known them had been complaining about wet Junes and Julys began to wonder when it would end. The pavements began to crack in places. Streets I had walked on all my life began to grow strange blooms in the crevices. The stalks would ease their way along the shopfronts and thick, oily, unrecognisable leaves would cover the plate-glass windows. And of course the timber on the railway-lines swelled, causing the metal to buckle so that the trains were later than ever. The uncollected bins festered but after a time grew strange plants too, hiding the refuse in rare, random shrubberies. So they had plenty to complain about, no doubt about that. For my part though, I didn't mind too much. I had always liked the heat. I took to wearing a vest only, under my suit, and walking to work along the buckled tracks. Those trains that did arrive I took advantage of, but for the most part I took advantage of the walk.

But then I've always been a little simpler than those around me. By that I mean that people somehow, even friends of mine—perhaps mostly friends of mine—would find plenty of chances to laugh at me. I had never minded their laughing. I accepted it. Things they seemed to take for granted I found difficult, and vice versa. Tax-forms, for instance, I could never fill out properly, so I would put them off until the writs began to arrive. Neither has gardening ever been my strong point. But give me a set of elevations, give me a thumbnail sketch, give me a hint of a subject even and I can work wonders with it. I often wondered: had my eyes been given a different focus to most others, so that while we looked at the same scene all right we saw quite different things? And of course people laughed, they will laugh, even get indignant, as when the tea you make is weak or you burn the toast only on the one side.

So when other people noticed the heat, what I noticed were the soldiers. I often wondered if they thought they could control the heat by having more of them around. Or were people succumbing to the leaden days in ways that were alarming? They were getting younger too, with that half-shaved look that kids have in their teens. Mostly on their own, never in groups of more than two or three, you'd see them keeping guard by the tiphead shrubberies, or walking the opposite way to everyone walking home from work, as if obeying some other plan. Is there a reason for it all, I wondered, that they don't know but that those who have plotted their movements know? And my memory of the time of my first realisation is connected with one of them.

2

THERE MUST have been a white bus that day. I didn't walk along the tracks anyway because I was walking up the roadway from the concrete path by the sea. I was walking up past all the gardens to my left and there was the sound of all the sprinklers hissing when I saw one of them inside the gate. He was as young as the rest, and dark-cheeked, bending over a rose tree. His khaki shirt was damp all over the back and under the arms. I could see his nostrils almost touching the petals. He is as alert as an animal, I remember thinking, or something inside me thought. There was the smell of just-cut grass. All the gardens stretched away from him, like wrapped boxes waiting to surrender the scents of their rose-trees. Then a door in a house opened and the soldier straightened himself, but not fully, for he slouched out of the garden and down the road. Underneath the rose-tree, I could see now, there was a pile of cut grass and a dog curled in it. I saw his long cheek and his glistening nostrils. They were flaring with the smell. Do they smell more keenly than mine, I wondered? Then suddenly I knew that they didn't. I was riddled with this extraordinary scent, moist and heavy, like a thousand autumns, acres of hay longing to be cut. I stared for a long time before walking to the house.

My garden curved, like a segment of fruit or a half-moon, from the gate to the front door. The house itself was square. It had been built in the days when houses were getting rarer and the ones that were built assumed ever-more-manageable forms. I walked through that curve of garden, past our roses, carrying that strange new sensation. I stopped then, just beyond the roses. I became conscious of a sound. It was a whispering, liquid and lispish, and it grew. I was carrying a briefcase, as I always do. I looked down to my left. All the gardens seemed to sing at once, a symmetrical hum of praise to that afternoon that would have been forgotten by anyone but me, and even by me, had the thing not begun. They curved away out of my vision and I imagined the last garden overhanging the sea, the same dullish hot blue that it had been for months, ivy trailing down a broken brick wall and touching the glimmering water. There must be a reason, I thought, the gardens are opening their pores. Then I walked towards the glass door, realising that the smell was cut grass and the sound was the hissing of sprinklers.

3

O F C O U R S E I wondered would Marianne's friends be there, talking about the heat, about the weather. I would not have been surprised to see, through the hallway and the open living-room door, the Ambroses sitting round our glass-topped table drinking weak coffee from our long, thin cups. I would have said something inconsequential, I suppose, and retreated to the conservatory to think. There I could look out on the back garden and watch the shadow creep round the sundial, the broad leaves of the knee-high grass glistening in the hot light, the garden which was by now a whispering, torrid tangle of olive-green. I could think there about the changes, without panic or despair.

But there were no Ambroses and Marianne was standing alone in the dark of the hallway. She glanced up when I came in and mouthed my name with that slight diffidence in her voice which was by now familiar to me. There had once been nothing diffident in our love. Her red hair was falling around the nape of her neck, so white that it always reminded me of china. She was turning and turning on her finger her band of gold.

Matilde is sick, she said.

I touched her neck, where the hair curled round it. She withdrew slightly, and shivered.

She's been calling for you.

Marianne walked through to the living-room. I turned upstairs and saw my fleeting shape in the mirror over the first steps. I stopped and walked back down. That shadow had for some reason disturbed me. I saw my shoulder enter the left-hand corner of the mirror and stared. I hardly recognised the stranger who stared back at me. Had I not looked for so long, I wondered. I stared for a long while and concluded that I mustn't have. Certain moods of self-loathing had in the past kept me from mirrors, but never had the gap between what I remembered and what I eventually saw been so large. Marianne moved into the living-room. Matilde called my name. I left my image then, carried on up the stairs and into her room.

Matilde lay curled on the bed, her hair tracing the curve of her child's back. I touched her forehead and felt the heat there. She turned and looked at me, her eyelids seemed heavy with the weight of her long lashes. The almond green of her eyes was flecked with gold. They stared at me, knowing more about myself than I ever could. She lifted her head slightly and her lips brushed the hairs on the back of my fingers.

I was dreaming of you, she murmured.

She seemed not yet out of sleep, or feverish. I could see my reflection in her pupil, ringed and flecked with almond. I was curved there, my cheekbones and forehead were large, the rest of me retreating into the darkness of her gaze.

Read me a story.

The stories she favoured were of unicorns and mythical beasts. She would drink in every detail of those creatures, the bulging arch of their brow, the skull the skin of which is so thick it could have been scaled, the luxuriant hair along each arm and palm of hand. So I read once more of the merchant with the three daughters, the sunken ship, the sea journey to the garden and the waiting beast.

After a while her eyes closed and her breathing became a long slow murmur and the blush on her forehead faded a little. I looked out through her window and saw the sun had vanished from the fronds of grass. I made my way out there and listened to the hissing of sprinklers from neighbouring lawns. I could see the mauve haze descend on the town, somewhere beyond my garden. There was the hum of night machines beginning, taking over from the last roars of day. I touched my finger off the sundial, so hot with the day's sun that it burnt the skin. I rubbed the burnt spot, noticing how hard it was. I rubbed finger after finger then and found each of them hard. Again I wondered how long since I had done this, or had this leathern hardness suddenly appeared? I looked around for no reason other than impulse and saw Marianne in the kitchen window, staring at me. I saw what she saw then, which was me, hunched and predatory, bending over a sundial to stare back at her. Her red hair glistened and her eyes shone. I shambled towards her through olive-green growth. There was the smell of burnt meat.

The radio was crackling when I went in. Let me help you, I said to her. I took the hot plates from the oven. Again my flesh stuck to the surface, but I felt even less than before. The meat was smoking gently and the smell of flesh drifted round the room. Sit down, I said to her. The word love, which I wanted to utter, froze on my lips. When I touched her neck, just where the red hair met the white, she pulled back sharply from my hand.

We ate the vegetables first and then the meat. The voice on the radio crackled on, bringing as it always did the slight panic of the outside world. Turn it off, I asked Marianne, but she didn't want to and so it drifted on like a voice between us, making our conversation for us. What is happening, I asked her after a while. I don't know, she answered.

While I washed the things, I heard her inside, tinkering on the bass notes of the piano. It was quite late by then, since we always ate late. I walked from the kitchen into the living-room. Can I play with you, I asked her.

She made room for me around the higher notes. We played the Chaconne in D minor, in a duet form we had worked out in the first months of our love. She played the bass as smoothly as ever, almost without a thought. My fingers found it hard to stretch, though, and an awkward rhythm crept into the tune. She was annoyed, understandably. She stood up swiftly after the end of the tune and lit a cigarette. I stared at

my fingers, which were still holding the white keys. I heard the
note hang in the air long after it should have died. Will you
come to bed, Marianne asked me.

We made love of course. I watched her undress and thought
of all the words to do with this activity. My mind soon exhausted itself. I took her white throwaway pants in my fingers.
She was lying under the featherdown sheet waiting for me. She
turned off the light. I buried my face in her paper pants, then
took off my own clothes.

There is a halo round you, she said. I looked down at myself.
There was light coming through the window. Each hair on my
body seemed isolated by that light like a bluish gossamer, a
wrapping. It is a trick of the light, I thought. I made my way to
the bed and felt her hand reaching out for mine. It rested on my
arms.

Her fingers were long and bony, but soft, with the softness of
her white neck. I had known them in so many ways, clutching
the pillow, rubbing my cheek, scouring my back, that the fact
that they felt different now didn't seem remarkable. Something
was happening, I knew, with us as well as with the rest of it. She
ran them down my arms and all the small hairs there sprang to
attention. I touched her eyes with my fingers, which miraculously seemed to have lost all their hardness, they were like pads,
responsive to her every pore. Her eyelids fluttered beneath them
and so I drew my fingers down her cheeks to the bone of her jaw
and down to that white neck. I leaned my face forwards and
kissed her lips. My mouth seemed larger than human, able to
protect hers in its clasp. I felt her tongue beating against my lips
and opened them and soon I felt her saliva in mine. My mouth
crawled down her body and she opened her vagina for me. Her
murmurs seemed to fill the air. Her knees were bent around the
small curve at the back of my head, pressing it downwards. We
seemed to twine round each other as if our limbs had lost their
usual shape. We made the beast with two backs then and somewhere in between our cries another cry was heard, a little more

urgent. Matilde was standing in the doorway, still in her dream.

You go to her, Marianne said, turning over. I rose from the bed and took her in my arms, which seemed no longer pliant, but heavy and cumbersome in every movement. Matilde whispered parts of her dream to me as I carried her to bed.

Marianne was asleep when I got back. I looked at my body in the dark and saw all the tiny hairs glistening in the moonlight. I began to dream, standing there. There was a skylight and the moon in my bedroom shifted above me, for I was a child, with face pressed to the skylight, staring down below. There were women, crossing and recrossing a parquet floor. Each woman carried a cup. The cups glistened with liquid. They entered a tiny arch and came out again with each cup empty. I inched my way down the glass to see better and for the first time noticed my shadow below, marked-out by the moon, much larger than I was. They noticed it too, for they all pressed into a circle and stared at me together, their raised faces like a large ageing daisy. The glass below me melted slowly and they each held a cup up to catch the drops. I melted in turn and an arm gathered me in a raised cup and a woman's face with two soft, feathered lips bent towards me to drink.

I awoke and the moon was outside the gauze curtain once more and Marianne was beside me, a swathe of crumpled blanket between us. Her slightly tilted nose and her upper lip jutting out from her lower looked strange, strange because once so familiar. How I would dream when we first met of that full petulant rose of her upper lip, the dreaming wistfulness it gave to her face. I would try to describe it in words, as if talking to a stranger. But no stranger could have understood.

I touched her long athlete's back and she shivered in her sleep, drew the sheets around her. She pulled away as if from a stranger. I looked at my hand on the white sheet that covered her white skin. It was much darker than it should have been. The skin was wrinkled and glistening, like the soft pad that is underneath a dog's paw. The nails were hard, thicker than they had been in the afternoon, the points curling round the tips of the fingers. There were five blisters there, from the burning of the sundial and the hot plates. I covered my hand with what was left of my end of the sheet and lay with my mouth close as it could be to her hair without waking her, my breath shifting the strands at ever longer intervals as sleep overtook me.

4

WHEN I AWOKE the sun was coming through the gauze curtains, cutting the air in two with a beam that hit the edges of the sheet wrapped round my legs. The dust wheeled in the beam towards the green carpeted floor. I heard the sound of the front door closing and of Matilde making her way towards school. There was the sound of clattering dishes and of the lawn sprinklers starting on their circular motion. Marianne came down the corridor and as she neared the room I wrapped myself in the sheet as a cover. I saw her in the mirror when she entered and she must have caught my glance for she turned and told me in that soft brusque voice that it was late. When she left the room again I rose. I kept my eyes from my body since sunlight is so much more revealing than nightlight. Both hands fitted through my shirtsleeves only with extreme difficulty. I dressed fully and slowly and made my way to the kitchen.

The moods that were between us were almost richer than speech. I sat watching her eat, eating only occasionally myself. However much I loved to watch her, I knew there was nothing I could do to dispel this silence. It had its roots in things done and said and it was like ivy now, twining round me. I spoke a few words, but my voice sounded harsh and unnatural. I then rose to leave and tucked my hands round my leather case, walking backwards towards the door. She told me that the Ambroses would be dinner-guests tonight. I will come home early, I said, and talk to you. There's something I must say. Do, she answered.

But what had it been that I had intended to say, I wondered,

when I passed through the gate and began the walk down the long sequence of lawns. The heat had brought a mist from over the waters, it clung to the edges of the lawns and the grass borders of the pavement. There was a steady movement of people from the lawns, down the pavement, towards the city.

The sea glistened from beneath the mists and I left the crowds waiting for the trains which I knew might never appear and walked along the tracks. Wisps of haze clung to the sleepers. I walked calmly, but inside me was building an unreasonable joy. This joy was nameless, seemed to come from nowhere, but I found if I gave my thoughts to it it answered back, asking nothing of me. It frothed inside me. The leather of my briefcase seemed moulded to my palm. I brushed back my hair. My tough nails scraped off my forehead and my hair leapt apart at the bidding of my fingers. The joy abated then and became still water. I knew I must keep it as much a secret as my monstrous hands. I heard a sound behind me and leapt back as a train thundered past.

I walked through the smoking piles on the outskirts of the city till the tracks tunnelled beneath the ground. I let the sleepers guide me through the void. I emerged in a long corridor of glass with listless crowds below, waiting for trains. I made my way to the silver escalator, which had been still for some years now.

In Nassau Street the tendrils of plants swung over the railings and brushed off the crumbling brickwork. The gaps between buildings gave a view of clear blue sky. The haze was dispersing now. I knew Morgan would be sitting in the office we shared, with his green eyeshade jutting from his forehead, his sharp observant eyes fixed on the drawing-board. I feared what those eyes would notice and so stopped off at a tailor's shop. I bought a pair of gloves, there, several sizes too big for what I once had been. I fitted them on behind a tailor's dummy while the assistant busied himself with labels. They made two large white, knotted lumps of my hands, more noticeable to me, I hoped, than to anyone else.

I reached our office in Crow Street. There was a games parlour downstairs that opened out onto the street. I saw the
screens glowing dimly inside, lit every now and then with flashes
of white, the shadows of youths bent over them. I made my way
upstairs to where Morgan sat, his eyeshade cutting his face with
a half-moon of green.

Having been partners for years, we talked very little. Whether
we didn't need to or didn't want to had become unimportant,
since it was comforting just to know each other's movements, to
be allowed room in another's presence, to work in alternative
rooms and make coffee on alternate days. We liked each other,
and I rarely heard Morgan complain about the heat. From his
window he could see the wide street spill over to the giant
building opposite where the paper-sellers would crowd with
each new edition calling the day's news. He would talk about the
quality of coffee I made, about the crossword puzzles and the
state of trains, but he would never question, senses of panic and
unease were unknown to him. He did the elevations, the line-
drawings, the fine-pencilled work. I would do the colours, the
storyboards, the broad sketches.

He told me a woman had called, and would call again later.
I walked past him and picked up, besides the acrid smell of his
sharpened pencils, the smell of something quite different. As I
entered my room it seemed to follow me, or I followed it. I knew
that smell, though I hadn't met it before.

I had been given details over the phone. She represented a
perfume firm who wanted to advertise a thing called musk. She
had described the associations she wanted the odour to carry in
the minds of the public. It was to be feminine, seductive, yet to
carry a hint of threat, like an aroused woman surrounded by a
threat she cannot touch, feel or even see. So I had sketched a
long rectangular drawing, almost Cinemascope in shape. On the
left-hand side was a white, porcelain bath. There were ornate
brass taps, a female leg crooked between them, dangling over
the floor, the rest of the body beyond the picture's confines. A

fine-boned hand was soaping the leg. Water trickled over the arch of the foot and gathered in drops at the perfect heel. The floor was patterned in black and white tiles, of which I'd forced the perspective a little, so the lines seemed to run like a web to the farthest wall. The dripping water from heel to floor then carried your eye over the chequerboard tiles to an open door and a corridor outside. On the open door was a gilt mirror. Full-length, turned in such a way that the bather couldn't see it, it reflected the corridor outside. And there I had sketched in a marble table, a telephone, a discarded bathrobe just thrown on the carpeted floor. There was an empty space, in the vague outline of a figure. That was to be the threat, awaiting definition.

It was odd to see my work on the boards, a product of yesterday's thoughts. I was different now, and found myself looking at it with a certain nostalgia. That threat, which seemed to be one thing yesterday, would be quite another today. I took my pen in my swollen hands and began to draw. Soon the pain of bending my massive fingers eased and the lines came. The lines of that fallen bathrobe seemed to clash with anything vertical and so I knew he would be prone, whatever else he was. I lined in a sinuous passive object almost touching the robe. The shape became bunched like a fist and the nails sunk into the carpet went deep, like claws. Hardly human, the curves of that bunched fist went backwards, always close to the floor, more a stretching leg than an arm. It began to rise then, with all the majesty and sureness of a sphinx. There was a torso there, waiting to emerge. I sat there, feeling it grow. It was all sensation, no line could have drawn its image. My back rippled and arched, there was a scent everywhere. There was the sound of a door opening.

She was wearing a hat, with a black fringe of lace round it. There was a small smile on her lips which showed that one upper tooth was cracked and angled inwards slightly. She walked slowly through the room, leaving that scent in the air behind her. I stayed at my board with my pen in my hands and my hands between my knees. I glanced at her every now and then. She had mumbled a word or two of greeting, hardly listening for an answer. She traced an arc round my things, picking up a sketch here and there and an odd finished drawing, the way professionals do, tilting her head as if to assess it, but already I knew her interest was more than professional. I find it difficult to explain how I knew this; my hands began to feel damp, as if they were sweating copiously under the bandages. Most of all it was the scent, which seemed to hang in the air like figures of eight. I felt that creature in my drawing in the empty shape in the corridor begin to grow, like a growing-pain. I could not yet see the form it would take, but I knew now that I would recognise it when it came, as I recognised that scent, which carried the name musk.

She pulled over the swivel chair and sat down beside me.

This is it, then, she said, looking at my drawing.

I said it was as yet only an idea. My voice sounded strange to me. Not so much hoarse as furred. I told myself I should not be embarrassed. But that scent, when she was close, was overpowering.

We need something extraordinary, she whispered. Things are so bad, firms are on the line. They want me to bring them a miracle.

I said nothing. I was a professional after all, not a miracle-worker. But I felt the pressure of something extraordinary, too extraordinary to be talked of. I felt a throbbing, like a pain, in my back, beginning in my left shoulder-blade, then creeping its way round my ribs. There was a knot of fur in my throat.

She changed from talk of the picture to talk of herself. I listened while she told her story. She came from the country intending to be a nurse but found all the hospitals overstaffed. I could see what a wonderful nurse she would have made. She had beautifully long bones in her arms and hands that folded with this restfulness. Her hair was auburn under the black lace and would have swung around her face as she bent over each bed and, together with those hands, would have given the bandaged heads a sense of heavenly reassurance. She told me how she wandered from job to job, mostly on the fringes of artistic worlds. Her tall figure and her auburn hair were considered a suitable adjunct to galleries and theatre foyers. She felt outside the events that went on there and yet people seemed to think, she told me, that she embodied their essence. Her present job had been foisted upon her out of the same misapprehension.

SHE HAD FINISHED her story. Her odalisque eyes were wide open on mine all the time she spoke. They were by no means beautiful, but they gripped me. I fell into the dream again, with the daylight all around me, I saw a long, golden stretch of desert. Nothing moved except occasional flurries of sand which rose in tiny whorls, as if filling vacuums in the air. The sand was sculpted in hillocks, which could have been the length of miles or the length of a fingernail. My eyes sped over these stretches, the outlines hardly varying till the expanse was broken by a jagged rectangular shape, pure black, sinking at an angle into the sand. It was marble, porphyry, or some alloy of glass. Inside I could glimpse a face, barely visible in that blackness of ice, hair frozen in statuesque, perpetual disarray. I had never seen the face before. One of the teeth was cracked.

She saw the half-drawn shape by the bathrobe as some kind of beast. I told her that was the obvious form for such a threat to take, but what kind of beast? She mused about it for a while, and began to enumerate species. I stopped her, telling her it was unwise to presume, one must let it assume a form of its own, one that we could never anticipate. She suggested a visit to the zoo tomorrow, to muse further. I agreed. She left then, tipping my arm ever so slightly, as if to impart some hidden message, or to imply some secret we shared.

I drew a few more lines. Soon my arms became extraordinarily heavy. My head was swimming with images. I let the pencil fall, let my arms hang by my sides and breathed deeply. Slowly and inexorably, the rush of joy built up. It was like a gathering wind. I sat there with my back slightly bent, my hands dangling and swinging gently as if to the sound of late afternoon traffic outside, the smell of musk in the air. The windows were rattling with the wind and beneath all sounds I could hear the deepest one, the one that was at the base of all sounds. I had never heard it before, but recognised it instantly. It came from below the building, from the earth itself. As if the roots of being stretched down, so deep down like a tuning-fork, and sang with an eternal hum.

Morgan must have come in then, for my interest was diverted and the joy slowly subsided. He had taken off his eyeshade, the first of the signals of his imminent return home. I rose from my chair. My arms felt light once more. Outside, night was coming down on the full street.

5

NIGHT HAD BEGUN to fall with a disturbing swiftness. Without any of the change from summer to autumn, around 1800 the sky would begin its wheel from cobalt to blue, and down in the streets faces, buildings and vegetable growths would be lit with a strange, lurid glare. It was the glare of changing, of heightened shadows, it threw darkened shadows under the eyes of passers-by. There was this yellow, febrile glow until the night lights took over.

The hot air seemed to enclose the crowds in a continuous bubble of movement. They arched their bodies, embraced, queued, made talk and love against the peeling brick. They seemed to glory, for a few brief moments, in the heat, in the sense of lost time and future. Their brightly coloured shirts and skirts moved towards me, the women indistinguishable from the men.

Morgan turned left at the river. I could see the bands of youths gathered outside the game halls. I could hear the buzzing of innumerable machines. I crossed the bridge. The crowds always seemed about to engulf me but clove apart as I approached. I suddenly felt older than any of them, older than anyone I could possibly have met. My steps became halting, my neck scraped off the collar of my suit with the roughness of what felt again like the pad beneath a dog's paw.

I found myself outside the station. The artificial palm fronds which passed me on the escalator seemed limp with the day's heat. Inside on the platform the crowds were there again, waiting for the train's arrival. The eaves on the corridor of glass above each held a drop of moisture which grew to fullness only to fall and be imperceptibly replaced by another. It seemed so much like rain, but I knew that to be an impossibility. And sure enough I saw a man in a blue uniform standing between the tracks holding the nozzle of a hose and sending a high arc of spray over the glass skylight and the artificial fronds alike. Walking on sleepers when the light is gone is foolhardy, I knew, so I stood in the shadows waiting for the train. The spray cleared the grime from the glass above and made the light and shade harsher. The man walked past me with his arc of water, dragging the pipe behind him in an arc of black.

The hall filled up with steam then and glass was obscured by billows of smoke behind which liquid flashes still managed to glint. In the shadows of the palm frond I rubbed my cheek with my left hand. I saw a series of tiny flakes twirl towards the ground, displaying a rainbow of colours in the half-light. I saw the crowds press from the platform into bunches round each door. I moved out from the shadows and pressed my way amongst them. I held my face down. I was disturbed at the thought of what it might reveal to them. Knowing how each one of us assumes that what is seen of him by others is not what he knows to be the truth but a mask, I felt a sudden terror that the whole of me was about to be laid bare. Whatever adjunct of our persons it is that maintains this demeanour, it was slowly leaving me, I realised that now. The skin of my person was being shed to usher in a new season, a new age. It would peel off me slowly and inexorably as if pulled by a giant hand.

My main concern, though, was that others should not see what I knew now to be the case. I pressed myself behind the last backs at the door nearest to me. I have always been considerate of others. My urge to spare their feelings will drive me to outlandish lengths. So I took my place some distance from the doorway, my face to the wall. When the train lurched forwards, our bodies swung to one side, then the other. The last of the evening light bled in both windows.

The movement slowly lulled us all. I felt the cramped space

between windows easing a little. I let my eyes take in the shapes around me. Bowed shoulders and heads led in waves to the window opposite. The angular city drifted by the glass, then gave way to the tips and heads of the outskirts and behind them a steady thread of blue sea. This blue slowly came to fill the window and to outline, and darken by contrast, the face that was nearest it. It belonged to an ageing lady. She had cascades of lines round her eyes and a fullness round the cheekbones that softened these with warmth. As the blue sea faded from the window a white, rich light slowly filled her face. She was remembering, I sensed. Her eyes were creased with those tiny wrinkles and had the wistfulness of everything that is best in humans. I knew I would either meet her again, or had seen her before. Then slowly recognition dawned. She was my mother.

6

I TWISTED MY body so I faced the opposite window. I heard a loud rending sound and several heads turned. I kept my face down, but from the corner of my eye could see that she had noticed nothing, she was in a world of remembrance all of her own. I remembered the poplar trees at the end of our garden and the plaid rug she spread beneath me. I looked down at my right arm and then my left. My sleeve had split below the elbow and the bandage was now in shreds. The change had spread to my wrist and then must have raced in a sudden surge towards the knot of muscle in my forearm. She would roll up the sleeves of her dress to let me count the freckles on her skin. I knew she lived upon the route but had never seen her take the train before. I would count the freckles till my eyes swam. My weekly visits had become an embarrassment of late with the gloom that swept over me in waves. I thought of how she must have missed me. In one full moment I felt how much I had missed her. My longing to touch her seemed to fill the carriage like a soaking cloud, like steam. A strange warmth rose from the whole of my body. I felt a dry rustle on my forearms and heard a soft fall on the floor, as if innumerable flakes were drifting downwards. I imagined them on the metal, in an untidy pile. They would be swept away on the return journey, perhaps by that porter with the water-spray. He would drown these shards of me without a thought.

I saw my mother's expression changing. From her window she could obviously see the platform approaching. The train halted and she left, with several others. There was more room, but I stayed pressed in the shadows. I imagined her walking down the blue-lit street towards the house I grew up in. I wondered would the time ever be right to call. I suspected it might not be.

My platform crept through that window, the train halted, I walked up the concrete steps. The liquid blue lay like a shroud over the tracks, the undergrowth beyond them and the rows of houses above. I walked, trailing my torn sleeve and bandage behind me.

The sprinklers were uttering their last whispers. Small piles of grass lay gathered beneath each rosebush. A dog barked from the third garden. A door opened and then closed again. I saw a car outside our house, with sounds coming from it. They were bright, chattering voices, so brisk and hopeful that for a moment I imagined they belonged to the Ambroses themselves. But as I drew nearer I heard the metallic crackles of the airwaves and saw the red light of the radio flashing on the dashboard.

7

THE FRONT DOOR was open. I heard voices coming from the kitchen. I walked quietly past, up the stairs and into the bathroom. My cheeks had begun to discolour in blotches, the skin ridged and bumped along them, puckered with holes. I put plasters over each one and I wrapped a long white bandage over my forearm, which was by now unrecognisable. Everything had changed or would change, I knew, and this knowledge made my efforts to hide it even more pathetic, and yet I pressed on with them. Such is the persistence of the human, I thought, and made my way downstairs again.

The voices seemed involved, like those on the car radio, in some common human drama. James's was the loudest and yet I could not distinguish the words. I heard a sound that was like an insect's hum for his, with an odd, irregular climax. I heard a more plaintive note for Marianne. Mary's sound I could not hear at all. I saw all three of them turning towards me when I entered. James rose and the hum became more and more irregular as if the insect was beating its wings fiercely, to escape. I avoided shaking his hand. I noticed for the first time how awkward his bones were, how he was all bumps and angles under his sleek black suit. His temple lobes were too long and his nose too sharp. Mary turned and smiled but her eyes were wide open in a stare that seemed as if it would never lose its amazement. Her pupils throbbed with the beating of her heart. Marianne looked up momentarily and smiled. Then the fringe of her hair covered her face as she held out a plate to me.

I heard all three sounds start at once, in conversation. There was tongue on the plate before me. I ate slowly, something of the flavour of the creature disagreed with me. James's hum throbbed on, swinging round towards me now and then like a pendulum. I heard the sound of Marianne's voice answering for me. It was soft, conch-like, falling like a wave, as if to protect me. I continued to eat. The soft threads of tongue on my own tongue made me feel as if somehow what I ate was myself. I looked up and saw Mary's eyes fall.

James hummed and rose an interval or two, then soared up an octave. Was it because I could not distinguish the words that I felt the need to talk? Or did his tone enrage me to the point of utterance? I knew I had embarrassed them, I knew it was all wrong, but I felt the need to tell them about the joy. You could not believe the joy of what has happened, I said to them, though everything may point to its opposite. Let me describe to you that unreasonable beauty that fills up my soul, unreasonable only because so unexpected . . .

I stopped when I saw my words were not helping any. There was absolute silence for a moment, then the sound of the tongue on James's plate being rent and lifted to his mouth. Then the sounds of conversation began again. They were coloured this time with a deep blush, as if with shame for something that had happened.

I rose with difficulty and excused myself. I crossed the long distance to the living-room door. The silence kept on. I closed the door behind me then and made my way across the hallway. I could hear the sounds raising themselves again. I went into the music-room. I looked at my bandages, which were now stained in places with a dull, rust-coloured liquid. I suspected I was sweating. I sat down at the piano and began to play. Though my fingers were cramped by the swathes I did get through, slowly and haltingly, the first part of the Chaconne. The long, full bass notes seemed to throb through the piano's frame, to mine, to the floor itself. I thought of the question, as I played, of why music soothes the restless soul.

I heard the sound of voices at the doorway, then Marianne's

footsteps back along the hall and the sound of a dinner evening ending. I stopped, I had lost the urge to play. I saw the liquid had seeped from my fingers onto the keys, staining the white ones with irregular threads. It made highlights on the black ones too. It looked like weakened syrup, but I suspected it might taste of salt. It was not at all unpleasant. I heard Marianne's footsteps up the stairway and the sound then of large, heavy rustling from upstairs. I followed, soon after.

The weight of my form must have shifted towards my head and torso, for walking up the stairs I had to grab the rails every now and then to stop myself falling backwards. The house was silent now but for a rustling of bedclothes somewhere and the tiny hum of Matilde's breath. I stood on the landing, listening to the new quality of this silence. Slowly it came to me that silence was not what for years I had supposed it to be, the absence of sound. It was the absence, I knew now, of the foreground sounds so the background sounds could be heard. These sounds were like breath—like the breath of this house, of the movement of the air inside it, of the creatures who lived in it. They seemed to wheel around me till I heard a piece of furniture being pulled somewhere, too much in the foreground, and the spell was dispersed.

I knew I must wash myself before the next move. Now was not the time to approach Marianne, and when that time came cleanliness would be essential. The bathroom, like that of most of our neighbours, was our pride and joy. The taps were gleaming silver, with handles and spigots elaborately wrought, with an elegant adjustable arm fixed to one side, holding a shower nozzle. The spray that came from this was fine and hard, with a lever at its base which changed the water gradually from cold to the sharpest heat. I thought of the countless times I had stood beneath it, in a different season, and the water had stroked me with its heat, washed away all the grass cuttings till Marianne sometimes joined me, her hair bundled beneath a cellophane cap, closing her eyes with pleasure and pain at the heat and her mouth puckering as she did so, waiting to be kissed. I would kiss her and let the water palm us both and her eyes would open as much as they could under the streams, her spare lashes looking like drowned kittens, her fingers, each one, edged into the ribs on my sides. The kiss would last until the hot water ran out and it would be a test of each other's endurance to wait through the cold till it came back, for the heat came in cycles.

So I remembered as I undid my hands how it was she who taught me to be excessively clean and how there are some lessons one should never unlearn. Now my hand was not my own, I saw the ridges and tufts of flesh come clear of the bandages, the hair matted with liquid and the muscles like scallops leading up to the forearm. I peeled off the other hand and the rest of my sodden clothes and ran the bath as I did so. The shower water would be riddled with memories; I thought I was wise to bathe in preference but discovered my mistake when the enamel filled enough to still the liquid and my reflection became clear. I had come to accept that I was not myself but had no conception of the enormity of the disparity between me and the being who confronted me. He was arresting, without a doubt, his forehead was tall, his nose broad and somewhat pushed in as if some afternoon, years ago, it had been broken in a fall. His hair was luxuriant and thick and swept back in clumps from his crown. His eyes were almond-shaped, fronted by even bushes of hair, white round the edges of the almond, streaked a little with red, then amber, gathering into black. Beneath his neck, which was ridged with two angular tendons, was a sharp V, then a scalloped expanse which swept in sharply then to his stomach which in turn swept in towards a tiny whorl. Beyond his stomach my vision was blocked by the edge of the bath but that was enough to see what a piece of work I had become. I stepped into the steaming water and dispelled my image with ripples. I found my changeable limbs floated with a strange buoyancy and took no stock at all of the heat. It filled them with ease, dispersed all thoughts of strangeness from me, everything found its place.

How natural it seemed to loll in that water, to turn and face the air again and turn again. The steam rose in the darkness like versions of myself and the lapping water seemed to echo round the lawns. I held it in my monstrous hands and let it drip down to the whorl on my stomach, where it gathered till it spilled over my flat sides. I couldn't have noticed the door opening, for I saw a shape in the corner of my vision then, a white shape, and it seemed to have been there some time. It was Matilde, in her nightgown. By her wide-open eyes, I knew she was still in her dream. Her dreams of beasts were never nightmares, for her stare had all the fascination of a child for an object of wonder. Her eyes travelled down the length of this body that jutted in and out of water, that filled her dream, that perhaps even was her dream. A knotted hand clutched the edge of the bath and she blew soft air out of her lips to ruffle it. I raised both hands and turned her then in the direction of the door. She walked out that way as silently as she had come.

I heard the rustle of her bedclothes and her turning over to sleep. I raised myself from the water and hammered the bath with the droplets that fell from me. I searched for a towel in the dark, but could not find one. I walked outside into the hallway and lay down in the thick carpet, letting it absorb the moisture. I turned on my back, then on my front, stared back towards the bathroom door. It was open. The gilt mirror fixed to the door-way held the reflection of the bath, but none of myself.

Within minutes I was dry. I rose and walked down towards the bedroom. The corridor seemed shrunk, as if the angles had become forced in upon each other. Through the bedroom door I could see the moon behind the gauze curtains. Marianne was asleep on the bed, the blankets rolled tightly about her. She had thrown two blankets onto the floor at her feet. I reached out my hand to touch her shoulder, but saw its texture against her white skin and withdrew it again. I rolled myself in the blankets at her feet.

WHEN I AWOKE Marianne was above me. She had thrown more blankets down, whether because of the excessive heat, or from the impulse to cover my shape, I tried not to think. I had all the appearance of sleep and so didn't move when she threw one leg over my shoulder to stretch for her stockings. I watched her cover herself with pants and then sheath each leg with nylon and saw her breasts vanish under a brassiere. She raised both hands in the air and drew on a flower-patterned blouse. She slipped her feet into two white high-heeled shoes, then drew her heels back sharply, grazing my cheek with a metal tip. She wrapped a kilt around her and walked from the room.

I lay on. I had awoken, but my dream was still with me. The moon shone through opulent French windows onto a parquet floor. The resinous gleam from the floor was similar to that over which the women had traced their circles. I was suspended from above, swinging inches above that gleam. The hairs of my cheeks brushed off the varnish. My eyes followed the rope which bound me, a vertical climb up to a creaking pulley, then a long sagging angle away. My eyes followed the rope down that angle to the floor, where it was knotted round the heel of a high-heeled shoe. There was a leg in the shoe which gave it weight and substance, immensity even, and yet strangely fine proportions with its line of ankle moving smoothly to the swell of calf. I swung my body on the rope. I rocked myself in ever-widening arcs towards that heel. I held out my arms to grip at the ankle but could never quite reach. Then the foot walked off abruptly, as if its owner was tired of waiting. I was swept quickly to the ceiling. I shattered the skylight through to the moon.

Marianne came in again. She unwrapped the tartan kilt from around herself and pulled on a skirt instead. When she had gone, I pulled the blankets down. My body responded only slowly to my efforts to move. My veins seemed sluggish and all my muscles seemed grossly overstretched. I made it over to the wardrobe and sought out my largest suit. This was a dress-suit, with adjustable buttons for waistcoat, jacket and trousers. I found a white starched shirt-front which I tied around my neck, since none of my shirts, I knew, would cover me. The problem of shoes I solved by slitting the sides so wide that my feet could splay through the opening. I then tore one shirt into strips for use as bandages, since my stock had quite run out. I waited then till I heard Matilde leave for school, then made my way downstairs.

Marianne was sitting with her face to the window. There was coffee across the table from her, with a bowl for me. I sat and ate as quietly as possible. She didn't turn or speak. Her red hair fell away in strands from her cheekbones. Her mouth expressed both hurt and horror, but most of all a kind of outrage. When I had finished the bowl I got up to leave. She turned her face towards me as I was at the door. There were tears rolling down each cheek.

She asked me how I could do this to her. I replied that it was not me that was doing it. Again the sound of my voice made me not want to say anything further. She said she would like to kiss me, but could not bring herself to. Will I kiss you then, I asked. When she nodded, I walked towards her. My shadow reached her first. I bent down and brought my lips to her cheek. Her tears moistened my lips and brought them some relief. I stood up then and thanked her, and made my way to the door. I didn't look back.

Such is the complexity of the human, I thought, as I made my way to the station. My appearance attracted attention, but I kept my eyes rigidly ahead. Anger, pity, love, hate, the names we give to our emotions signify a separateness, a purity that is rarely in fact the case. She had stared with anger, pity, love and hate. I walked, again, along the buckling tracks. The sea was leaden today, like a pit of salt, with only a little mist. The fronds of the artificial palms, when I came to them, were still fresh and erect after their night watering. Morgan's eyeshades touched the drawing-board in greeting when I entered.

I sat down to work. I began with tiny details, put the major questions quite out of my mind, and as often happens when that is the case, the details themselves began to answer the questions. I filled in the highlights and shadows of the enamel bath. This led me to her leg, which I lit with an almost porcelain finish. The shadow fell from an unseen light-source, cutting an angle between the side of the bath and the carpeted floor. I followed the tuft of carpet the way one does a wheat field, with a series of vertical strokes nearest the eye, followed by a ruffled expanse. The sun was falling on the left-hand side of my face. I rubbed my cheek occasionally, because of the itching of the heat, causing a shower of flakes to litter the page, which I each time duly blew away. And in this way I was led to the figure. He extended himself from the tufts of carpet, with a shape that was indeed sphinxlike, two noble paws pressed deep into the pile. Sphinx though seemed too common a name for the creature he was becoming. I teased my mind as I drew with names for him, but any others that occurred seemed equally inadequate.

I had him half-sketched when I suddenly broke off. I found myself exhausted without knowing how or why. The sun had nearly crossed my drawing-board which was, I surmised, more than two hours' journey. I remembered my appointment. I rubbed my face and snowed the drawing once more. I went to Morgan's room, but he was out. His room was eerily silent, as if he had never been there. I decided to walk.

I wrapped my bandages round my hands, arranged my shirt-front so it covered the widest possible area and ruffled any further flakes from my hair and face. I then borrowed Morgan's eyeshade, the shadow of which I hoped would be more than enough to cover my visage. Then I ventured out.

HOW LONG WAS it since I had walked between morning and night? The city seemed to curl under the sun like a scalded leech. The shadows were tall and black, the pavements white and empty. I crossed Westmoreland Street alone, the only movement the rustling in the patches under the walls. Is the world to be left to me, I wondered, and such as me? A statue of hot bronze pointed nowhere, his finger warped by the years of sunshine. I walked through the sleeping city, blinded by the glare, meeting no one. I came to the river, which had narrowed to a trickle in its caked bed. I walked beside it up by Parkgate Street. The Wellington Monument jabbed towards the white haze, I passed through the parched Hollow towards that long avenue, whose perspectives seemed to beckon towards splendours unseen. I saw then, after some time, a shape approaching out of the melting tarmac. I heard the clip-clop of hooves and readied myself to spring into the bushes, in case I met horse and rider. But no, it was a deer which walked down towards me and stopped some feet away, as I did, to stare. I noted the grace of his rectangular jaw, the dapples that led from it to his sprouting horns. Do you see things differently from me, I felt like asking, are your perspectives wider than mine, have you two planes of vision to carry everywhere you go? Whether I thought this or phrased it, he seemed to hear, for his lower jaw moved at odds with his upper and he bounded past me, in two neat, languorous leaps, as if inviting me to imitate him. I merely watched him, though, disappear into the city haze.

As I walked on, the shape in front of me defined itself. I could see a glittering white façade with two proud pillars and the whorling fingers of a wrought-iron gate between. Walking further, more pillars defined themselves, white ones, stretching in pleasing harmonies from the façade of the house. It slowly dawned on me that it was the presidential palace. Then the memories came. They flooded in on me, like the dreams, the avenue was full of them. I leaned against a slim tall tree, with no foliage at all except for an umbrella at the top. I saw my mother, walking towards it. She was wearing a narrow pleated jacket, with a flowered skirt. She was walking down the avenue, holding my hand. I was pulling her towards the hedge beyond. She wished to view the palace from behind the gates, but I wanted to see—what was it I wanted to see? The zoo, I realised. And I stepped out from under my tree-trunk, remembering. Enclosed by those hedges, I remembered, the animals would leap at that tall barbed wire, lining the path to the presidential palace.

I crossed the avenue and walked along the hedge. I heard a few mournful snarls, as if of creatures woken for the first time in years. I came to a turnstile and walked through. The Swiss-style cottage was still there, but now it gave out no afternoon teas. The wires were everywhere covered in ivy, the bars were twined in eglantine, honeysuckle and in thick trembling vines that lined the roofs of the cages. I walked through the empty zoo and heard a few parakeets squawk, I saw the flash of a pink flamingo rising from a pool, I saw a treetop swarming with small green monkeys, but all the great animals seemed vanished. I felt a sudden wash of disappointment and realised then that I had come here to find my beast's prototype. He was no cousin of those chattering monkeys or those squawking birds. I came to a pool then and saw a ripple break the covering of thick green slime. A seal's shape curled out of it, its back speckled, even coated in this weight of green. His glistening, troubled eyes made me feel more akin to him. Then he dived and left the surface unbroken once more.

I was walking through a tunnel of vines when I heard footsteps. I bent beneath the hanging branches, as fearful as before.

The gardens were free now, to animals as to humans, and yet my fear kept me cowed. There was the dusty odour of evergreen leaves. Then another scent crept through it, the scent of quite a different place. I ventured out to those approaching footsteps and recognised her walk.

She was carrying a black handbag, swinging on the crook of her arm. She did not seem to be aware of it. She was wearing a fawn hat which made a circle of shadow round her face. I swear I could smell the perfume from where I was. Her high heels clacked and clacked as she walked nearer, her eyes searched around constantly. She was on time, I gathered, as I must have been. When I stepped out in front of her path, she didn't show fear or surprise, only a familiar gladness.

I took her arm without any hesitation. We walked through the vines and out the other side, where once there was a reptiliary. The shed skins of its old inhabitants lay scattered about, colourless and wafer-thin. Her heels clattered off the tiled floor. She told me more about her life, but asked no questions at all about mine. Why I found this so comforting, I wasn't sure, but walking round the glass cases, my arm fell about her waist and hers around mine. We came to the exit sign and walked through, finding ourselves on a long green lawn. Even under the rolls of bandage and under her cotton dress, I could feel the bones of her hips and the movement of her skin above them. We sat down on the lawn.

Take it off, she said, pulling off my eyeshade.

Don't you mind, I asked, feeling drops of sweat fall down my outlandish forehead. She had a matter-of-fact air, however, that made such questions seem redundant.

You look tired, she said.

I was tired. She took my head between her hands and laid it on her lap. She stroked my forehead and my matted hair then, while talking in a deep, hypnotic voice about the project and herself. While she talked, although my back was to her, I could see the limpid shapes of her eyes before me. She talked of the complaints of everybody around her, of the hundreds of minor dissatisfactions they gave voice to daily. She herself, she told me, felt a dissatisfaction that was deep, but that she knew would never end, so what was the point in voicing it? She told me how heat appealed to her, she could wear light cotton dresses and always kept a colourful supply of wide-brimmed hats for going out in the sun. She told me how her life to others seemed to follow no shape, since she never worried or guarded against the diminishing future. But she said that the fact was that while she did accept most of what happened to her, she would have a premonition of important events some time before they occurred, as if to prepare her for them, so she could take advantage of them. She had felt that when she first heard the name musk.

I turned my head and looked up into her face. I put my hand on her knee as I did so. Take it off, she said, and began to unroll my bandages. I protested, but she whispered, in this persistent voice, that it could do no harm. She unwound it and unwound it till the first hairs began to appear between the white, and then the huge fist was exposed. She put my hand on her knee then and wrapped my elongated fingers round it. I felt her whole knee in the cup of my hand.

She told me more about herself. I could see long machines cutting corn in swathes as she talked. She talked of herself as if she were describing an acquaintance she had known for years, but never well enough. There was a girl, I gathered, before the woman. The thought that we all had some past was becoming difficult for me. But looking at her I could see her face diminish into the other she must have been. She stretched out her leg so that her knee straightened under my fist. Some bright green-coloured birds flew out of the cedars. I felt her knee change shape once more as she bent her long leg at an angle under my chin and began to talk about the beauty. My voice sounded deeper than ever and so I turned my head to see if it had alarmed her. What I found was her eyes staring wide at me in a way that left no doubt that each was understood. I told her about the sounds I had discovered beneath the surface of things, the hum from the girders, the mauve twilight. As the surface of everything becomes more loathsome, I said, thinking of the thing I was, the beauty seems to come from nowhere, a thing in itself.

She leaned towards me and again I knew I had been understood. But the pleasure of that thought brought an anxiety with it, as to whether she had been. She took my face in her hands, she was smiling. How long was it, I wondered, since I had felt uncalloused skin against my own? The beauty came in a rush. Joy was the word I thought of, joy I knew then was that word for when beauty was not only seen or heard, but felt from inside. The sound of it was all around me. Her eyes were the brown of burnt heather, with tiny flecks of gold in the dark. They glowed as she bent her head down towards me and rested her lips on mine.

The green birds must have flapped closer, because I heard their cries, one after the other so that they became a throaty purr. How I admired her boldness, in meeting my lips which must have changed beyond recognition. The rest of me must have learnt a new suppleness, however, for while still lying on her lap I managed to turn and raise her above me in the same embrace. Can I describe the garment that wrapped round the top of her legs? She murmured again and smiled, and again I thought of her descriptions of herself as not herself. She gave a small cry as of a bird released and all the green parrots flew into the air at once. Her limbs wrapped round me, each one seemed interchangeable, always with the same texture, and I knew then that I had a soul for she met it, embraced it and breathed on it with her own. We lay there, brute and beauty, a small curtain of pollen seeming to fall on us as if cast off from the blue skein above. There was a dry flowered smell.

It was some time before we rose. My soul had twisted itself into a knot that it would keep, forever, I thought. We walked back through the arboured tunnel. Her heels clicked once more against the path. She told me that the insides of her legs were wet. She rested her hand on the crook of my arm. Behind us tiny animals followed, unseen, only present by the noises they made, small whispering and rustlings as if to celebrate the hour that had passed. We agreed to revisit the reptile parlour, then to go for the time being on our separate ways.

Even as we walked through the shattered awning, I was made aware of further changes, by the minute. The skins of dead reptiles hung off the vines and as we walked beneath we set them swinging, collapsing the remaining panes into shivers of crystal. How wise of that genus, I remarked to her, to cast off a surface with each new season. She rubbed her nail up and down my forearm and told me more about her childhood.

I listened as she talked about books, how an unlettered farm girl would remove them from a large tea chest beneath her father's workbench and phrase to herself the long words, few of which she understood. They seemed a secret knowledge to her, and when she came to work in galleries, her surprise at the fact that others shared it was only matched by their surprise at the freshness her childhood knowledge had retained. Several times I tried to answer but found my voice retreating once more to the deep cavern of my throat. As the words went, then panic came that the essence of that hour we had spent was vanishing, shedding itself in turn. She turned to me suddenly, as if noticing this, on instinct. It is time to go, she said.

Before leaving she wrapped me carefully once more. We left by different entrances. I walked back down the long avenue and knew that each change that happened was reflected in that bowl-like essence that lay somewhere beneath the skin. The avenue was empty of people, the shadows slept at the feet of the trees, long and somehow full of ease. My feet moved over the grass, faster and then faster, I felt abandoned beneath those trees and dared to move out into the open fields. I saw a mark on my wrist and made out a number, in stately blue ink, barely smudged. She had written it there. Everything would be for the best I felt, having no knowledge of what awaited me.

TRAVELLING IN the mauve light at the irregular time that I did, the train was quite empty. The city barely rippled in that light, the soldiers had left it, the water lay still to my right like a sheet of well-tempered glass. My vision was obscured with a fringe of hairs to the left and right of the oval it had become. I sensed this was caused by the growth round my temples. But it lent a charm to that seascape, fringed by rainbows that threw into relief that gunmetal blue. Then all the light bled from the carriage, my shadow came to match the tint of the metal floor. I felt suddenly darker. The train lurched on its sweep forwards, as if dragging me towards some Armageddon.

And small gusts of spray blew over me when I came to the gardens. There was wind at last. I thought of the conversations that wind would make around evening tables. There was a slow dull pain in the palm of my hand. I looked down and saw that my fingers were curled like clams. I had mislaid my briefcase.

The front door was ajar. I made my way through the house. I could hear Matilde or Marianne or both moving round upstairs but I didn't call. I felt they had heard me. Something moved me through the house and out of the French windows onto the lawn. I stood by the sundial amid the mounds of cut grass. I felt Marianne's eyes approach the window upstairs but didn't turn or look. I tried to imagine what she must see below her, but no effort on my part could make that leap. Sure of what I felt like, all images of what I looked like were beyond me. Was I rotund, I wondered, did these luxuriant clumps of hair spill out from the crevices of what served as my garments, intimating the chaos inside? Or was the hair in fact quite sparse, did the flakes that I left behind me like gossamer cover my cheeks, my fingers, every centimetre of available flesh that wasn't hidden by cloth? I remembered that my skin at times had made her uncomfortable. Did she remember that now, I wondered, and then realised how futile it was. All I could gauge was that whatever creature was filling her gaze had his left hand placed upon the disc of the sundial, the two largest fingers supporting the weight of his leaning body. I didn't dare return it. All I could bear was to call her name, my eyes fixed on the digits of the sundial, and wait for a reply.

I must have waited a long time for her voice, because when I became aware of my surroundings once more I was encircled by a halo of tiny insects. They hovered over the dial's copper surface, then up along my forearm, into a lulling, shifting crown around my head. The light that came through their penumbra was green, that strange pea-green aura I remembered from the first days of spring. Their combined hum was like the murmuring of angels. Their eyes were bright and green, and to my huge blue the magnificent swathes of their wings reduced to just that transparent glimmer. I remembered a glen, and her red hair surrounded by them, her long fingers flicking them from her face. I took my fingers from the sundial and began to walk back towards the house. They followed me, like a retinue all of my own, but then they thinned as they approached the French windows, as if their proper home was outside. I entered the house with some sense of loss.

There was no meal in the kitchen. Once more I waited. I stood by the range feeling that to impose myself any further might be a mistake. I sensed a presence and heard a footfall behind the door, but could only see the door's gentle swing and the ghost of a shadow on the floor.

Have I become repugnant to you, I wanted to ask, as gently as the tilt of that door. But I feared the sound of my voice. So I waited to see would she enter, of her own accord.

The shadow departed and the footsteps retreated up the stairs. I kept my silence for a moment, and then thought of

Matilde. The longing to say goodnight made me move once more. I crossed tile after tile of the kitchen floor. The scalloped shape of the soles of my shoes no longer suited my posture. I would have thrown them off and walked barefoot, but felt that would have worsened things. I pushed open the kitchen door and felt the resistance of tiles change to the softness of carpet. As I reached the banisters there was a rustling above. I heard her voice.

Don't come up, she pleaded, Matilde's not asleep.

Please, my darling, I said, but the words sounded like heavy drops of oil, don't be afraid. I want to kiss her goodnight. I would have said more but I could feel her fear rush down the stairs towards me like a wall of water. I could by no means blame her, but that fear served to goad me even more.

Matilde, I called, hoping I could pronounce at least that. Marianne's sob answered me from above.

Come up, then.

The top of the stairs was bathed in light. Marianne was there, a spiked baking tin in her fist.

Say goodnight from the doorway, she said.

Your voice, I tried to say, sounds as foreign as mine must be. Again the words curled beyond speech. I walked up slowly. She kept her metallic shield thrust towards me. I placed my palm against the spikes. The landing seemed unnaturally narrow. I followed her covered hand to a door.

Goodnight Matilde. I attempted the syllables slowly. The broad *a* reminded me of a field of grass and the *ilde* made me think of a thin bird flying directly upwards. I tried to picture both of these as I phrased her name, the thin bird flying directly upwards out of the sea of grass. To raise the timbre of my voice I contracted all of my throat muscles.

I heard no reply. I drew as quiet and deep a breath as I could and began again. Before I reached the first consonant, however, I felt a blow from behind. The metallic spikes scraped me like a claw, I fell headlong, I heard a door slam and a key turn in a lock with a short reverberant click.

11

THE HOUSE FELL into its evening mood, that mood of which one might remark how quiet it is. On the contrary, it was a harvest of sounds. I lay with my cheek on the carpet and listened. I knew now that I was not in Matilde's bedroom but in my own, or, to use the terminology of the past, our own. My fingers touched off a gossamer substance which seemed for a moment or so to be castaways of mine but which I discovered, as I pulled it towards my lips, to be a long silk stocking. I drew it through my lips and the smell of her skin came to me with a strength that it never had had before. I recognised the odour of the drops she added to her bath. Woman and the world that word implied seemed as strange a bestiary to me as the world I had become. I listened to the sounds and tasted the memories that smell brought to me. The moon was swelling into the rectangle of the window. I was in a bar with oak and gold-coloured fittings, waiting for her entrance. There was a door adjoining which led to a dancehall, and dancers surrounded me, some awaiting their partners, others already joined. I stood a little on my own, as if to express the pride I felt, knowing that when I held her in my arms I would want no other. I glimpsed myself in the bar-room mirror, quiet, saturnine, but above all, proud. They surrounded me in couples but none would be as beautiful as she. Then she came in, wearing what she called her disgraceful dress. It was white, glittering with spangles, slashed all over with half-moons that showed her flesh. The dark silk of this stocking glowed beneath it, flashed black as she moved towards me and one leg parted her dress's sheath. We kissed at the bar, before the mirror, and moved towards the dancehall;

even before we had approached it our movements blended into dance. We wove through those thousand couples and that perfume was our own.

The memory of that perfume was easier than her name. One by one the lawn sprinklers stopped their hissing. The insects that had thrived on the long heat beat against the window-pane, lit by the globule of blue light that the moon had become. The perfume waned and ebbed in my senses through the chorus that I once thought of as silence. My arms were tough as beetle-hide beneath me on the carpet. My lids were heavy but took a long time to close. Slowly, though, that chorus changed from bluish to black and I fell asleep.

12

THERE WERE curtains of dark like curtains of silk, the blackest furthest away. There was one lone hair on an expanse of tan, which swathed off from me like a desert. At its base the earth swelled a little like a pore, then sucked inwards. And as I stood there it grew. Grew so much that it bent away near its tip, under pressure from its own weight. A tiny drop formed there, fell away and splashed at my feet. I began to walk over that undulating surface, through the curtains of dark. What had seemed darkest from some way off melted, as I approached, into the hue of what I had left behind. There were no humans in this landscape, though all about me was the aura of humanity. The darkness dispersed as I walked towards it, then formed again in the middle distance. I felt I would meet a woman here. Another smooth basilisk grew some way off, soaring from its pore beyond my field of vision. Around it grew neighbours, too smooth to be a forest, too separate to be a field. A drop splashed beside me, so large that it wet my ankles. Then another fell and another, so much so that the water rose to my waist, surged in a current and drew me away. Its colour I would have registered as blue, had the light been clear enough. I hardly swam, I was borne with it over that landscape that sank under its even progression. There were threads of hair beneath me, stroking my body like moss or water weed would, but of a more silken texture, long, flowing with the water, as if each strand was endless. I dared to put my feet down and felt the fleshy surface. I walked to a bank and raised myself up. The water ran below me now, the hair wafted with the flow. There was a woman some yards beyond me, on the bank. Two great webbed feet caressed the woman, her hair made fury with the water. All above me was the beating of wings. A white neck curled from the sky as if on a sudden impulse, its predatory beak turned this way and that. Was it the sight of me, I wondered, that made the sound of wings more furious, that caused those feet to rise, that white neck to coil about that woman, bearing her upwards? Her hair dragged itself from the yards of water and soared, whipping my face with droplets before it was gone. The bank from which she'd risen flooded with water, forming a pool. I made my way to it and bent. I saw my monstrous head reflected there, ringed by a circle of eggs. Were they the swan's, or the woman's, I wondered and lifted one of them out. The heat of my unruly paw was anathema to it, for the droplets of water began to sizzle and steam and a crack sped across the white surface. The sheaves of egg fell away and a cherub stood there, creaking its downy wings. One by one the other eggs split and the cherubs beat their way to the ceiling. They settled into niches in the plasterwork. There was the sound of falling water.

13

WHEN LIGHT finally spread over the contours around me and the clusters of colour gathered at each eyelid I found I was on the floor no longer. The bed was beneath me and the sheet was crammed into a ball, shredded in parts where my fingers had clutched it too ardently. There was a sound in the air which I could not immediately divine. I got to my feet and it was all around me, a steady thudding like the feet of many children. I went to the window where the light was. My eyes were unsteady as yet but when I pulled back the gauze curtain and gazed out on the unfamiliar, I saw it all. It was raining.

The water came in straight threads, the darkest ones furthest from my gaze. Had I dreamed that liquid, I wondered, from the constant sky. But I saw that in the gardens all about me the sprinklers had stopped, and gathered that others must hear it too. There was moisture in the air, that scent of dryness had vanished. My bandages clung like a mask.

There was the sound of a table being laid downstairs. I was not at all hungry. I squatted, held my knees close to my chin and listened to the downpour. Each echo that came from downstairs was different now, muffled by the falling water. Towards evening I heard music and the sounds of guests. I rocked backwards and forwards by the window. There was a rhythm to the falling water to which I responded. A kind of sleep came.

I dreamt I was in the room downstairs. A metronome ticked from the piano, with the sound of dripping water. I played, keeping my fingers on the black notes. Marianne stood above me. Matilde danced, in her confirmation dress, the white frills spreading as she turned. The liquid beat spilled over the piano though and soon my hands began to sweat. My bound fingers stretched for the notes, so that Bach was slowed to their shape. I knew it was going badly. Can we not try it again, I asked Marianne, but the russet stain was creeping from the black notes to the white, making them indistinguishable. The liquid thud from the mahogany frame began to wilt then, to melt into a gurgle. Matilde turned bravely but the wafer-like stiffness of her confirmation dress became sodden in turn. It hampered her movements, it clung round her knees like whipped cream. She twirled and twirled, but could not defeat it. Her tears made matters worse and soon her Crimplene elegance was plain grey, clinging to her sides. The greyness oozed from the keys, the same as the colour that bound me, and soon music, room and all of us were buried in its path. I saw their hair, twined just above that matter, in the shape of a fleur de lys. It bound and unbound itself as if in final parting, then too went under.

THE RAINS MERGED day into night and night into day
again. The dull throbbing and the whispering of rivulets
outside and the distant cascades of trains enveloped me. A light
fungus grew on the walls, a furred coating of gossamer. I would
loll against this vegetable surface, my breath wreathing the room
in billows of steam which dripped in tears from the ceiling. So
my room wept at intervals and the carpet vanished beneath a
film of grey. My lungs, like sodden sponges, inhaled their own
moisture. At intervals a plate was pushed through the door. I
ate, but hardly noticed the textures. Each dish grew a web of its
own. I slept and woke and slept again, lulled by those watering
noises. My limbs ceased to concern me. There was a kind of
peace in this moisturous world and I wondered once how it was
regarded by the world outside. Morgan's eyeshade would be
dispensable, I gathered, since the hard sunlight was no more.
The streets would have changed from a dusty tan to a shimmer-
ing grey. I dreamed that perhaps my condition might have lessened. Then the rains stopped and I knew that I could dream no
more.

THERE WAS A calm, willow-green evening light. All the drops had finished but their liquid echo lasted for some time. Old sounds gained precedence, old but fresh because so long unheard. There was the crackle of burning fat from below. A plate clattered. Then came the hissing of sprinklers, like barely discernible strings.

I rose, very slowly. My limbs stretched at their coverings, having grown in the interval. I knew there would be no reversal. Certain tendons felt like wads of bunched steel. I walked to the doorway. It was locked as before but I gouged round the keyhole with my nail. The wood splintered easily, the door swung open. Now that crackle of fat sounded louder and the pall of singed flesh slowly filled the room. But stronger than that was the pall of memory. I heard the front door open, the sound of voices, of entering guests. The door closed again and the voices fell to a murmur, broken by the occasional soft ringing of glass. I stepped onto the carpet. I thought of my appearance, but looked in no mirror, as mindful of my own terror as I was of theirs. The landing, which had once been planes and angles, throbbed as I walked through it, the ceiling seemed to congeal beyond me into a closed mouth and yet raised itself as I came forwards, as if parting its lips to let me through. The stairs whorled below me in turn. I followed the glimmer at the end of them, through which the sounds seemed to emanate. My fingers gripped the rail and my new hands left palm marks on the cedar wood. There was the door then, tall, soft-cornered and ringed with light. I stopped, listening to the voices. I meant to enter, but knelt first on the carpet and put my eye to the keyhole of light. I saw the dim shapes of figures round a table. Then the handle turned, the door fell from me and I collapsed inside.

There were kitchen tiles by my cheek once more. I saw the foot of Marianne, the long black heel rising to her ankle, and her hand, clutching the doorknob and her face, far above me. Her voice was raised, but the words I could not distinguish. I understand your anger, I said, I have become an embarrassment to you, I can see that clearly. But from my prone position on the tiles those words didn't sound like words. My darling, I tried again, perhaps it's better that I leave. Through the curve of her shoe's instep I could see that table, the dinner-lamp hanging low and the Ambrose couple, male and female, staring towards me with curved, craned heads. Marianne's foot rose and fell again, nearer now to my eyes. I inched backwards away from it as I felt I should. It rose again and the heel sang off the tiles. I gathered myself onto all fours. Do you remember that evening we danced, I began, but that heel numbed me into silence. I craned my head round and stared up at her face, which seemed larger than a full evening moon after wet weather. Should I go, I mouthed and the eyes, though they didn't seem to hear me, seemed pregnant with the word Yes. I backed away and sidled round the doorway, still longing for a contradiction. But the heel clacked off the doorway and the doorway clacked shut. I heard the rustle, the regretful whisper of the key turning. I raised my weighty palm to that door and gouged some words on the cedar. Goodbye.

THE DARK HAD brushed all the gardens outside. Each lawn swam with what the rain had left and the cuttings of grass lay like moss upon the surface. I walked. I was watched only by the moon, which shone silver above me, swollen, as though it could contain any number of dreams. When I reached the tracks a few restful stars had joined it. The sleepers had swollen into giant sponges and between the lines of track, glowing dully with the rust it had gathered, a steady stream of water ran. I found night so much more comforting than day, each shape seemed like a disguise, each shadow a mask. A reptile slid down towards me through the waters, passing under my legs to the sleepers behind me. The city, when I reached it, gleamed with the metal of new rain. I walked along the river, glistening at last, laced with ropes of fungus and the pads of lilies. The bridge barely curved above its growth. It seemed now hardly necessary, the river at points spawned a bridge of its own, vegetable and massy, beneath which it remembered its liquid state. There was the steady moan of travelling water and a film of moisture followed its curve to the bay, and beyond to dimness. My feet padded over the metal bridge and their muffled echo seemed to come from beyond. A fish leapt clear of the lilies, gripped a moth in its jaws and plunged downwards once more. I walked, with no knowledge of where I was heading. Somewhere, I felt there was a place for me. And the bridge led me, as it only could, to the empty street alongside. There was a cobblestone archway ahead. A tangle of foliage hung from above. Through the olive-green leaves I saw an edifice glowing. I brushed the leaves apart with my arms and walked on towards it.

A S   W I T H   C R E A T U R E S   whose bone structures enclose
their flesh, ants, crabs and armadillos, lending support
from without rather than within, so the girders of this structure
bound the planes of concrete and glass. It was square-shaped,
beetling over the tiny streets around. It threw more a mood than
a shadow on its environs. Not a soul walked on the pavements
around it and the mists, which were now dispersing elsewhere,
seemed to cling to the brickwork for comfort. How had I not
noticed it, I wondered, in what I was at last beginning to think
of as my former life. I had the dim memory of waiting under that
Dutch-style façade beyond for a cream-coloured bus. How long
must that have been, I wondered, and how long did this immensity take to build and under what conditions of secrecy? It was
a seat of some power, I sensed. The surface of the brick was
smooth, even metallic, and it tingled gently under the pads of my
fingers as if to give just a whisper of the power within. The mists
rose to my waist, close to the wall. I walked along it, feeling that
tremulous whisper. I reached a corner. It was sharp, seemed
dropped like a plumb-line from the stars. I could then see large
steps and a concrete patio leading to the miniature street. The
dimensions of that street, once so snug and human, now seemed
absurd. This giant that scraped the stars had winnowed any
purpose it might have once had. There were vast globes on the
patio that lit it from the front. The building rose beyond their
beam though, and vanished into gloom. The steps rose to plate-
glass doors, higher than any human frame. They would have
sufficed even for me.

I walked back beyond the corner to the girder-point. I
removed the bandages from my palms and I began to climb.

Soon the mist was below me, and the patio, and the street. My cloths unwrapped as I rose. They made white flags in the breeze beneath me. Then even the clouds dispersed and the moon rolled yellow next to the clean line of brick. My shadow came with it, darkening the streets. The stars pricked the sky all over, the moon ladled over them and the wind whipped round my loosened limbs. It tore at my bandages, set them free then in one long roll from my waist. I had come to the end of the girder. There was a parapet above me. I paused, clinging with both hands to an overhang.

The last piece of white unravelled from my calf. I let loose one hand and grabbed the cloth with it, swinging freely. I was naked, I realised, but observed by nothing but the moon and stars; for one moment my body sang. I hung on, and each tendon felt at home. I looked up at the moon and whispered a sigh of thanks. The stars glowed brighter for a moment. I heard the wind and the furling of cloth. I let my eyes follow the bandage, which billowed in a long white arc, drawn into a curve by the high wind and tracing figures to the ground below me.

It was no longer empty. A small boy stood there. His hand was stretched in the air for the white end. It hung above him, moving back and forth. I considered what he would have seen and felt proud of myself, his eyes watching. He had the calm concentration of all children. I let the bandage go, as a message or gift, and swung myself in one movement over the parapet.

I thought of wheat fields at night, their yellow tips gleaming as the full sweep of the night sky came into my vision. All the stars had cleared themselves of mist for me, like hard bright cornheads waiting to be gathered. I balanced on that parapet without much difficulty. My toes gripped the edge while my heels still hung over the void. There was humming in the air. It had two pitches, bassy below and thin and wavering above. Did it come from those stars or this building, I wondered. I let my eyes fall with it from the wheat fields to what lay at my feet.

The roof was of plain cement with a spiral staircase jutting out into the skyline. Many yards away, near the opposite parapet, was a rain trough. I stepped down onto the roof and felt the cement beneath my feet.

The staircase was made of thin steel which sang when I plucked it. It made a dark half-segment through the roof. I climbed down, into the building below.

I found a long, low-roofed storeroom. There was a rolled carpet against the wall. Through the slim rectangular windows the wheaten stars could be seen. I crawled inside the cylinder of carpet and was soon asleep.

18

MY DREAMS were of humans. I was smooth once more, my hair was cut close to my temples, I was wearing a suit I had never seen, it is tighter in fashion than in my day I remember saying. Absolutely unfamiliar with myself, like one who has drifted off and been suddenly woken in mid-afternoon, I knew obscurely that what I carried under my elbow, pressed to my side, was a brief of some kind. I walked down a long corridor with flowers on the floor, there were sweeps of light coming through successive windows. When I came to the fourth door I knew that this was where my assignation was, though there was no indication that doors down the long corridor beyond were any different. I knocked, heard no answer but entered anyway.

She was standing by the window with some beads on the high-frocked dress which gave her figure the repose it had always promised. She was twisting the beads in her fingers. She did not look up when I entered, allowing me to see to the full what a woman she had become. The creature I had left, so small, so unformed, with those long ribbons of years ahead of her, had emerged, both bound and unwrapped by them, the child I barely knew so changed as to be almost hidden and quite another creature revealed.

Matilde.

She turned when I called her name. Like those exotic birds in whom, by reason of acquaintance with their more prosaic cousins, we recognise some characteristics, I could see in that long neck, in that tiny ruffle which seemed to spread from it to the crown of her short cropped hair, some ghost of her childhood movements.

She came towards me and kissed me. The kiss was a brief one, but in the quick withdrawal of her face from mine I sensed a torrent of emotion. I looked into her eyes and saw them at once angry and pleading for kindness. I knew then she was in love, she had been in love and felt mishandled. I felt pity, but even more, a sense of great misplacement that her body had touched another's, her soul had met another's. She called me by a name then, not my own, and it dawned on me that she was in love with me.

She asked me to reconsider my feelings. She told me no one but me could fill her life, now or for a long time to come; perhaps forever. My coldness she could not understand, but she could live with it if I were to give even a hint of my former affection. Nobody could have been like me, she whispered, during those moments.

I wondered what I had done, how I had met her, how I had kept my identity secret. But the light that came through the great plate-glass window from what seemed to be a workaday, silver-lined city outside imposed its own order on my words, my movements. I felt the great ageful wash of guilt, I must have known, obscurely, in the pit of the consciousness with which I performed whatever acts I had performed, who and what I was. It inhibited my words even more. She was bathed in that light, so proud and vulnerable, shifting backwards and forwards, her tall comely shape like a product of it, so statuesque and proud, waiting for words I could never utter now I knew who I once was, what I later was, to her. At last she took my silence with finality. She became as shapely, as functional as that light.

The light surrounding her was oblong and tall, suiting her proportions. Then the light changed and all the angles softened and I was staring now at a circular orb as rich as morning. There were rainbows in front of my eyes and the multitudinous curve of those hairs once more. Like sedge-grasses or rushes sweeping down a dune, they glistened with pinpoints of moisture as if Morning herself had bestowed them upon her, sucked through that invisible line between light and dark. I knew then it was my arm, on which my large head was resting. The long funnel of carpet was up there, a mouth of light. The morning sun filled it almost totally, distorted only by the grime on the plate-glass window. I stared at this sun for a long time. It as golden as ever, but no longer an orb. It was blessedly elliptical, as if the lenses of my new eyes had given it depth. Then the sun was eclipsed by a shape that entered its curve abruptly and hung there, wavering slightly, its edges blurred. Was it cherub or flying creature, I wondered, hovering just beyond the edges of that plate-glass; until it spoke then, and in a boy's voice.

I brought you your things, sir.

The voice was high-pitched and eager, with a slight hint of the Americas. I wondered what being would call such as me sir. I dragged myself towards the light. His face withdrew somewhat, then approached again. A hand stretched.

I kept these for you. The way you climbed that building was really something.

His hand was firm and surprisingly strong. It grasped mine until I clambered out. I rose to my full height and stretched myself. I could feel his eyes on me constantly, admiring and awestruck. I almost shared his wonder at my movements. The air was cut in half with the light which slanted in one rigid plane, darkened my upper half and lightened my lower. There was a plain white marble block by the window. I sat on it, my knees became half-orbs of grey. The marble was cool, chalk-smelling. I placed my chin in the palm of my hand and looked up from the repose of myself to his face.

I kept them for you, he repeated. They're as good as new.

He held the bandages in his tiny hands. The first stirrings of haze began in the city behind him. The bandages were amber-coloured; last night's rain had sullied all the white. He held them out as if presenting a gift. And when I took them from him I felt the mood of my last self rise like steam off them, they carried an odour like the juices of a thousand memories, if memories could

have been crushed like grapes or rose petals. I let them drop to
the floor and a cloud of dust rose from them, as if they were
unwilling to say goodbye.

Is there anything you'd like? he asked.

I had been reluctant to speak, remembering the loathing that
my voice once produced. But I trusted in his trust of me. I told
him slowly and carefully that yes, I did feel hungry.

What do you eat?

And I realised for the first time that I was not sure. I had the
memory of what had once been a tongue shredded on a plate,
and of murmuring voices. Had I not eaten since then? I told the
boy I was not sure. He described, his eyes wide open and eager,
the various kinds of foods that he could get me. His father grew
sweetcorn in the basement, where the heat from the immense
boiler that he stoked let them grow to "that size"—and he
stretched out his arms. There were leftovers from the office
canteen. He could even get me whole dinners, at a pinch.

I imagined the broad green leaves of the sweetcorn and so
asked him for that. He ran to the door then, but stopped there
and turned. He stared at me. His brown eyes seemed almost
embarrassed.

Is there something wrong? The timbre of my voice was by
now like whole forests. His eyes flashed towards me and away.

I want to see you walk.

So I rose from the marble block and took his hand in mine
and walked to the plate-glass window. Every tendon seemed to
stretch like never before. The light filled me when I reached it.
I let go of his hand and pressed both arms against the glass. The
glass, which transmitted such heat, was itself like ice. My forearms blazed with colour. I turned to see was he happy, but he
was gone.

I felt the light come through me. I walked up to the spiral
staircase and climbed outside.

19

THE CITY HAD grown its coating of haze, so thick that the skyline imitated a horizon, an even murky blue, but for the largest buildings which soared above it. Periodic gusts of hot winds spread across it, dragging me now in one direction, now in the other. I was drawn towards the cement pool and there saw myself again, with wonder now and a touch of delight. The water was miraculously still, maybe four feet deep. I was fawn in colour, strange elegant angles like curlicues whorled where my elbows were. Underneath the tawny sheen my limbs seemed translucent, changed into some strange alloy, gelatin perhaps, opaque where the bones might have been. I could have stretched for an age. I slid into the water then and assumed its element. Threads of gold flowed out from me, shifting with the ripples. I rolled my head under and around and came to the surface again, dreaming of that hair again that flowed towards a bank. Two great webbed feet were splayed above it. There was the sound of flapping wings, the sky was muddied by white and the feet slowly rose, underneath the bales of beating feathers. A large egg rocked there, backwards and forwards. A line streaked across its surface, then a regular crack which grew, emitted small bursts of chalk dust. The sides of egg split, two wings struggled to light and a Phoenix head above them, a jabbing, mareotic beak turned this way and that. It grew to fullness then flew, again the flapping bales of feather drew the webbed feet upwards. The fragments of shell tumbled into the water and hissed there, bubbling gently. Something green floated among them. I gripped it between two fingers. It was a head of corn.

The boy stood by the pool's edge, his thin arms folded round a host of green corn-tips. He smiled and I saw for the first time a gap between his teeth. I slid from the water to the pool's edge. I ate the corn slowly and he ate one too, as if to share the moment with me. I peeled the broad green leaves which the wind whipped away over the parapet into the haze beyond. He told me how the corn struggles through its envelope of green and only throws it off when it attains perfect ripeness. Has that happened to you, he asked. I answered that I could not be sure.

He told me then how his brown complexion came from stoking the enormous stoves which powered the building which his father, the boilerman, kept under his charge. He had stoked them for six years, and was now aged twelve. He asked me my story and I told him of the changes, the bandaged dinner-parties and the escape into the night. He nodded, and seemed to understand. I remembered Marianne and Matilde, and standing by the sundial underneath the fencing, and my cheeks moistened with tears. I felt a pain where my heart should have been and my shoulders began to heave with uncontrollable sobs. He put his hands on my temples and laid my head on his minute shoulder. He told me of dreams he had of changes, that his father was in fact a king who lorded over quite a different building in a large suite, serviced by a glittering lift.

Will nothing bring you back? he asked.

I told him I was not sure. He spoke to me then of wizards, of magic potions and maiden kisses. He kissed me on the fingers, as if to see could that effect a cure, and his eyes took some time to change from hope to disappointment. Then he confided in me that his disappointment would perhaps have been greater if I had changed back since nothing could be as splendid as what I was now.

There was a rumble in the building then and the liquid in the pool broke into ripples. That sound started up, both high and low at the same time. They were the boilers, he told me, starting up for the day. He would be needed to run errands and stoke them. Was there anything else I needed?

And I remembered her then. Like a clear liquid that one drinks with very special meals, the taste brought back that perfume, that dark hat moving among the drawing-boards, those long knees in the reptile house. We had both shared the changes. My longing to see her was as sharp for a moment, as brutal, as all that had happened. I held my pliant wrist, remembering the bandage she had written on. I told him there was a number, written on the bandages down by the carpet-roll, could he ring it and tell her I was here.

I saw him run across the large empty slabs below, the white bandage streaming after him. He stopped at the edge of the street to roll it in a ball, but it unwound when he ran on again, trailing through the morning crowds. I sat on the parapet, feeling somewhere that I should think of things, but my thoughts resisted any shape. Each minute brought a mood of its own to which I succumbed.

So morning passed in a series of changes. Every moment presented a different vista. The winds blew in one and died down in the next. The sun kept its heat but moved perceptibly, bringing all its shadows with it. All the creatures of the air seemed to cling to the shadows and move with them too. Towards noon they settled as if the heat had lulled them at last and they knew that the shadows, decreasing since daybreak, could only grow. The pool steamed gently. I began to walk. I paced around my rectangular home and the creatures rose in flurries with each step. They seemed to anticipate each of my movements and cleared the warm concrete under my feet before each of my footfalls. I paced the concrete for what seemed an age. Each brick was infested with life. More creatures whispered from the crevices in the parapet. I stared over the edge at that great sweep of concrete and glass, and that whisper became a roar.

There was the sound of footsteps and I turned as she emerged from the spiral staircase. The wind came from below now and tugged at her dress and the straw basket she was carrying. The boy came out behind her. He stood watching as she walked towards me past the pool. I stood with my back to the parapet. She had a flowered dress. A stick of bread jutted from the basket. I went to move but none of my muscles would answer. The wind lifted her dress in gusts like the bowl of a hyacinth over the stems of black stocking which covered her knees. I felt strangely transparent under her gaze, as if she could see as she approached every cranny of me, down to that strange heart of mine still woven into a bowl from that afternoon of animals.

My darling—

She held out her hand and touched mine. Slowly the whole of me rose to attention. The boy stared from behind her. Her only expression was a smile.

You are different again.

She drew me down beside her to tell me about the world. The company Musk had gone bankrupt, the product vanished without trace. And Morgan? I asked. She had called three days in succession, she told me, found the office closed and then transformed into a manicure salon. Do things change so fast out there? I asked. Everything, she answered.

I thought of Morgan and how our years together would vanish without trace. The wind lifted her hair and transformed it utterly.

Can I embrace you? I asked her.

When she smiled in reply I put my arms around her, felt how they stretched with ease down below her spine to the tops of her thighs. She stroked my back, which seemed to mould itself into her hand's movement. I could picture the shape it assumed, a scallop, ridged to its base by her five long fingers. She drew one finger from the hollow of my temple down the long plane of my cheek and buried it in the golden strands of my torso. I lifted her in both hands, one beneath the small of her back and the other behind her knees, and walked with her to the parapet. She laid her cheek on the concrete and her eyes followed each one of my movements. Behind the flame of her hair the city steamed in its haze. My largeness was apt at last, my three fingers stretched the fabric of her dress, they exuded a warmth that filled her eyes, I was nothing that I had ever known or imagined. I carried her to the pool and dipped her slowly just beneath its surface. The green corn-leaves floated everywhere, clinging to her body as I lay with one arm stretched on the bank, the other rippling the water. She made a crown of thick dark olive with the leaves. And as she played with me I changed, the hair of my forearm became sleek and shining, my fingers bunched like the feet of cattle. She nudged against my ear and drew one arm around me, wrapping the long strands of my tail about her neck. The boy made a wide fan of the corn-leaves and beat the air repeatedly to cool her. We played all afternoon under the boy's slow, quiet eyes. They filled with our delight and delighted us in turn. I saw a band of gold glistening in the water. I brought it to the surface and saw it was a wedding-ring. Long, slow tears coursed down my face then. She brushed them clear with her hands, but they kept on coming. And as if they understood my need, they held me while I wept, filling the pool to its brim, tears spilling over the sides. By evening, the whole parapet was wet.

She left with the last of the light. It held on barely, very barely, while she travelled down the core of the building. I saw her make that short, hesitant run across the piazza below and onto the empty street. The darkness slowly filled the air behind her, as if only my gaze had been willing it back. The way the inky blue of Matilde's palette gradually merged with and swamped the pink, that way the night invaded each yard of street as she passed over it.

20

THE MOON THEN came up and spread its own brand of light, and its image in the water was rippled by the wind. I was content to lie and measure its ascent and observe the gradual appearance of the stars. The spiral staircase became etched with silver. In my naivety, my joy, I had neglected to ask either of them about what lay below. That anonymous hum which even now persisted seemed to imply any number of worlds. I made my way to the staircase, swung myself onto the whorl of metal and crept downwards. I saw the concrete room and remembered my bedding in that roll of carpet. Below that again I found a hall of wires. They spread in all directions, all shapes and colours, from the tiniest to cables the circumference of my torso. The humming, so anonymous above, had grown a certain depth down here, as if each wire carried its own note, from the thinnest soprano to the basso-profundo of the thick-set cables. I thought of the music of insects, so ravishingly conveyed to me that garden afternoon. Each sound then had seemed bred of chance; no graph, no logical architecture, could have determined the glorious chaos of that chorus. But here, purpose seemed to reign. The wires sang in unison, with a constancy that had an end in view, an end I could only guess at.

The end must have been in that building, or perhaps the building itself was an end. With this in mind I made my way across the hall of wires to what had the appearance of a lift-shaft. The array of white buttons was discoloured with age. Too small for the pads of my fingers; I had to press them at random, several all at once. I saw hawsers glisten through the metal grid, I heard the clicking of grease and the whir of a motor. And then the trellised box of the lift rose towards me.

We sank downwards through the building, the lift and I. Those dim halls rose to my vision and away again, each much like the one before. The buttons I had pressed must have determined our passage, because we stopped, unaccountably, in a felt-lined corridor without much distinction. I stepped through the trellised doors. I was half-mindful of going forward, half-mindful of going back again, when the doors slid closed. The lift whined and the light on the panel sank downwards.

I walked forwards. There were doors off this corridor, with rooms leading to more doors. What I had assumed to be devoid of life I soon found to be a bestiary. A deep-piled room seethed with mice. A moth watched me from a filing-cabinet. His eyes, full of the wisdom of ages and the fierceness of his few hours here, seemed to require my attention. My ears swelled with a sensation I could hardly feel as sound, let alone speech, and yet I felt from his quivering wings the urge to converse. I brushed him onto my palm. His glance seemed to harden—with disdain, it seemed—and his wings beat their way skewwise towards the doorway.

I followed. His uneven flight, irritating but somehow alluring, drew me down stairways, passages, lit only by the fierceness of his glare. We were now in low-roofed concrete tunnels, similar in texture to the ones I had left, far above. He blundered into walls and cables, but somehow always kept ahead of me. Then that jagged flutter changed to a spiral of panic. I heard an unearthly trill, like the vibration of a toughened tongue in a mouth of bright leather. I turned and saw the scythe-like wings of a bat swoop by me, then change its flight into those jagged arpeggios the moth was now weaving. They traced each other in counterpoint for a moment and it seemed a second cry rang out with the bat's, a cry that was soft, like the sound pollen would make brushing off a wing, but yet a cry with more pain in it than any I had heard. Their paths merged into one then, the bat's mouth opened, then closed, and the bat flew on alone.

The corridor seemed like a tomb to me afterwards. That ashy cry seemed to echo down it, bringing tears to my eyes which made the walls glow. I made my way to the corridor's end, hoping for a lift or concrete stairs. The tunnelled walls curved and were lit by a glow that seemed brighter than the rainbows of my tears. It was yellowish, it flickered, there was a rhythmic, scraping sound. I heard voices then, one old and masterful, the other young. I came to the corner and saw the boy in the distance shovelling coal into a furnace. The heap he shovelled from was replenished from a source unseen. His shovelling was too tender to keep his heap down to size; it kept growing until it almost engulfed him. He was goaded on by shouts, coarse and violent. Then a dark-skinned figure in dungarees appeared, shovelled furiously with him for a moment, sent him spinning towards the furnace with a blow and left again, admonishing him to work faster.

21

WHEN THE BOY appeared the next morning with his arms full of cornheads and that glad expression on his face, I didn't mention what I had seen. I breakfasted on the corn and watched the leaves whirl over the city on the early-morning wind. Even that wind seemed to partake of the savagery of last night's events. The mists slowly disappeared, revealing the tiny beads of the morning crowds. I bathed in the pool and as he washed each sinew, I noticed weals on his body where before I had been aware only of that dusky tan. I questioned him on the rules of the building, though. He told me that he worked by night, and by day the building fed upon the heat he had generated. The corridors were peopled by secretarial ranks and the whir of office machines took over from the more ancient machines of the night. I asked him was he tired by day and he told me that he was, but the pleasure of my presence kept him awake. I told him that once my presence brought very little pleasure, to man or to beast, and he answered that he could not imagine how this could have been so. After a time he slept in my waterlogged arms. I wrapped myself round him, to accommodate his dreams.

I awoke to find her standing above me. It must have been early afternoon. I whispered at her to be silent and placed him beneath the shade of the parapet. We became lovers once more, then many many times. The concrete bubbled with our perspirations and we took to the pool for refreshment. She floated there, staring into the sky as I told her of the bat and the helpless moth. She told me that life had its own laws, different for each species. Does one law not rule us all? I asked her. How can it, she answered, or else we would have seen it. I asked her was there a law for me, as distinct as those for the bat and the moth. If there were, she asked me, would you obey it?

I had ceased to think of thoughts as thoughts, for the effort to separate them from the clouds of sensation that germinated them was mostly beyond me. Now, however, I pulled at this thought, I needed it clear, abstract and separate so as to find an answer. Her head played around my armpit then gradually fell asleep. I remembered dimly a tale of a beast who cried to the world to reveal him his destiny, to send him a mate. If there was a law for the bat, for the moth, for the woman, there must be a law for me, a law as succinct and precise as those laws I obeyed when walking past the whispering gardens each day to work. But how to find out this law, and the destiny it implied? But then, it occurred to me, walking by those gardens, along the torrid tracks, I had been no more aware of what law I obeyed than I was now, obeying no law at all. If asked then, was there a pattern, a plan, I would have said no, categorically no. So law, if law there was, revealed itself in retrospect, like a sad bride coming to her wedding too late to partake in it.

My efforts at thought exhausted me and these fancies gradually sank into that well of sensation from which they had emerged. The darkness seeped around me, like a torpor brought on by my mood. It was indeed night. She still slept in the niche of my arm. I lifted her head and placed it at my navel, and curled around each of her limbs to make her sleeping easier. The wind ruffled her tangled clothing and set the down along her cheekbones alight. I thought about what laws bound us and she opened her eyes then, as if in answer to that thought. Her lids parted slowly to reveal my curved reflection in her pupils. I stared at myself for a time, for perhaps too long a time, seeing me, seeing her, seeing me in her. Only when her eyes were fully open did I become aware of her expression. She took a sharp intake of breath. The horror filled her limpid eyes as the night had filled mine. She drew backwards. I raised my hands to clutch her, too roughly. Please, I whispered. It's the night, she said, you're different. No, I cried. She was standing now, walking backwards towards the staircase. You should never have let me sleep, she whispered. The dark moulded her like a curtain, her hair glowed like sullen rust. I can't help my fear, she whispered, you should never have let me sleep. Her hand searched for the metal staircase. No, I whispered again, but my whisper gathered like a roar. She ran from that wall of sound. Somewhere above me, stars began to fall.

22

I LAY FOR A long time. The darkness weighed on me. Who would remember the extraordinary length of her legs, I wondered, who would delight in that softness of skin at the joint of her knee, if not me? The changes came with such rapidity. Was the air never to be still, I wondered, from one moment to the next? To whom could she tell those stories, of the large tractors swathing through the meadows, of the young girl walking through the dew-soaked stubble? And even now the pace of my grief was such that I could feel it entwining me in a skin of its own. She had seen something, I remembered, something that caused the fear, and I rose slowly to my feet and staggered to the water. All I saw there was a shadow, like some more essential shade of dark than that which surrounded me. And I managed the thought that even what she had seen was now part of the past. Yet the desire to see what she had seen persisted. I made for the building below, searching out a mirror.

The lift was made of trellised bars of metal. None of its surfaces conveyed the ghost of a reflection. I pressed the buttons for some level below. I heard the whine of the motor, and with it a sound that was not a sound, that was above sound, that was a sensation, around my skull, my cheekbones, like the needle-points of a sandstorm. I raised my hands to my cheeks to locate it. Then this sound took shape, flowed into vowels and syllables, into sentences. It spoke.

You operate this lift, it said, like someone remembering what it was to travel in it. And yet you look like—

What do I look like? I asked. I closed my eyes. The voice began again.

You take your texture from whatever surface you inhabit. In this lift you belong to that odour of grease, hawsers and trellised metal. Outside it, I would have no idea.

I opened my eyes. I saw opposite me, clinging to the bars, a bat. His eyes were bright with reason. I remembered the arpeggios of fear and the death of the moth. That leatherish mouth didn't move, and yet his voice sang all around me.

Can you fly? he asked.

I shook my head.

Each animal function, he told me, has its sister emotion. Loathing, he said, has been your companion for some time.

He moved his head and seemed to smile. Do you wish to fly?

I nodded.

Take us up, then.

I pressed the buttons. He stared as we swayed upwards once more, a stare full of brightness, whimsy, intelligence.

Hᴇ ᴄʟᴜɴɢ ᴛᴏ the matted hair on my arm as I walked from the staircase. I placed him on the parapet. His sightless eyes turned in their sockets. I could feel his voice again, prodding me like gorse. Forget wings, he told me. Watch!

He moved both arms as if stroking the air, stepped off the parapet and plummeted like a dead weight. I cried out in alarm, but saw his fall, of a sudden, transform into a graceful curve. It became a figure of eight and slowly drew him upwards once more. He hovered above me for a moment, full of cries.

Wings are quite useless, he said, mere symbols of our activity. Birds, being vainer than my species, love to proclaim their importance, cover themselves in feathers and tails they can fan. But all one needs to fly with is desire.

And I thought of how swallows always reveal themselves in spring like small threads of longing and as the heat grows they become rushes of memory, filling the air with their curlicues, never touching ground, symbols indeed of desire.

Do you desire? he asked me.

I had hardly thought before I flew. The parapet swung above me and the piazza grew larger, swam before my eyes till I left it behind and moved in a long curve down Dame Street, barely at the level of the second windows, piercing the rim of that layer of heat that the night hadn't yet dispersed. I took the breeze on my left side at Nassau Street and swept down that channel of air. Some instinct drew me towards the river. I felt his voice all around me again and glanced up to see him at my shoulder, his wings dipping easily and gracefully with my infant movements.

Lead the way, he whispered, so I swung him down the steaming river and then left, face above the railway tracks, under the long glass awning, through those arcs of spray that splashed on the night trains. We kept close to the rails as sleeper after sleeper sped below us, each like a resinous wall. I smelt the odour of cut grass then and rose and skimmed above garden after garden till at length I came to one where the blades had not been cut and recognized it as mine. I headed over the tips of the nodding grasses, barely able to see through the pollen. There was an immense triangle jutting from a metal plinth. I hovered over the heiroglyphs on the disc below and saw how the moon's cast upon time was at variance with the sun's. I saw a large ball of light somewhere up ahead. I left the sundial and made my way through the grasses once more. The ball of light beckoned through the clouds of pollen and then the air suddenly froze. I beat myself against it, but to no avail, the light was there, but sealed behind it, impenetrable. I had almost exhausted myself when I recognised the frozen air to be glass, the ball of light a flickering bulb. I slid downwards. A large jewelled palm wiped moisture off the pane. Through the swathe that was cut in it I could see a glass, half-filled with liquid and the same hand lifting it to the crescent space between lips. I was indeed home. I watched Marianne for what seemed an age, from below. In my absence her lips had changed from deep cherry to rust, her hair had been shorn tight, the corners of her eyes had grown two black triangles. Two fingers indented themselves on her cheek and the dome of another's head descended for another's lips to meet hers. I recognised James.

There was a letting-go and a sensation of ice sliding past my cheek. I fell down among the grasses below. Her lips, though larger to me than ever, were still those lips I remembered. Down among those roots of green I could still picture the kiss, too long, far too long for the desire that had carried me here. I tried to beat myself upwards but not a whisper of movement ensued.

I felt the air stroking my face then in soft hushes, and his voice sang round me once more.

You know now why bats are what they are, poised between strutting and flight. To fly cleanly you must learn pure desire, a desire that has no object. Any attachment to things of the world leaves you earthbound once more.

I held a pure blade of grass between my palms and imagined pure desire. I could picture nothing, and soon nothing was all I pictured. Slowly, very slowly, the memories left me. The house, the hissing sprinklers, the sundial. That window was the last memory to go, and the kiss drifted away like whorling water, and I rose, to hover inches over the lawn. He chirped with a pleasure that made me soar. Soon the house became a tiny dot in the palette of the blue earth below us.

THE CITY SANK, like a glass bead into a muddied pool. The air was pure above it, with the ethereal blue of a wedding-gown. He seemed not to move, but yet was all movement, rising above me. Desire, he said, when purified, becomes desire no longer. I felt his voice and soared with the certainty. Loathing, when purified, becomes loathing no longer. I felt all affirmation and drifted towards him, his eyes glowing sightless in the gloom. Through blindness, his voice sang out, we cultivate the vision, through sensation we reach it and yet what we reach we still cannot see. He drifted around me like a thread of silk. Yet the feeling, he whispered, is our only road there, so can we doubt that the feeling is all?

He drew his limbs about him and let himself fall. I fell to his pace, just above him. The air thickened and the streets billowed out below. There is a city, he whispered, to whose shape all cities aspire. And when the sheaves of our city fall away, we shall reach it. When will that be? I asked him. Tomorrow, he sang. He curled his furred body and sped downwards.

I STOOD ALONE on the parapet under the moon. Alarth—for that was his name—had vanished into the depths of the lift-shaft. The streets were empty and silver, like a dream that was now dreaming itself. I slid down from the parapet and walked towards the trough. I saw my face there, as limpid and clear as the moon beside it. Each breath I took was like a sliver of lost time. I inhaled and seemed to drink in hours. To each beginning there was an end, I knew, and each change hurried it nearer. I walked down the staircase to the comfort of the lift. I pressed the buttons and felt the gradual slide downwards. The cables of the lift swung, shifting their curves as they did so. I thought of the gardens, through the long heat and the rain, of Marianne's face with its triangles of black. That change, so miniature, had brought an ache to me as large as that the chaos of myself had brought to her. There was a law, I now knew, and its resolution would come to be. I pressed the buttons with the stumps of my arms. The door slid back and a corridor faced me, like all the others. There was no moonlight here to illuminate my way, but the discs of my eyes soon accepted the black and the dark became light of its own. A swarm of midges hovered round a door. I entered, and saw a room in the chaos that work had left behind. There were paper cups, the rinds of cheeses and a bottle of mineral water. There were drawing-boards ranged against the walls and across the slope of one of them a figure lay sleeping. I recognised the crescent of the green eyeshade and moved myself closer. Beneath the dull green shadow I saw Morgan's face, his lips immobile, a day or two's growth on his chin. He had vanished when she called, she had told me, and must have found different employment. I saw drawings crumpled beneath his head, those buildings of concrete and glass that had come to litter the city, half-finished. Conceived by nobody, it was generally imagined, and built in the owlish hours. Yet their source was here, in these immeasurable rooms. Spanning the wall behind was a miniature of the city as it once had been. I looked at those squares in their measured movement towards the river, their proportions so human, yet so perfect to the eye. I saw the park, etched out in strokes of green, the zoological gardens at its centre. I remembered the textures of pavements under my feet, of grass round my ankles, the doorways that once stared at my child's eyes, the balanced stone of their arches and the fanlights of glass. I saw drops splashing on Morgan's clenched hand and drew my lips down to taste the salt of my tears. The hand shifted then, the fingers stretched and touched my movable skin.

It is you, he said, after a moment's pause.

I nodded. His reddened eyes flashed under their arc of green. What is it like, he asked, to be away from it all?

I shook my head. If I could have spoken I would have asked him not to talk, reminded him of our days without words in adjacent rooms. He rubbed his eyes and gestured round the room.

Each afternoon, he said, I draw the city for them. And each morning my instructions change.

Who are they, I would have asked.

I work for them now, he added. He gripped a paper cup and began rubbing it to shreds.

Do you remember the time, he asked, when we used to work until five and walk down the river to our separate trains?

Yes, I said. The word came out round and true.

I sleep here now, he told me. I wake and I work and I sleep again. I keep the shutters down so that the light is the same.

I asked him would he mind if I pulled them back. He shook his head slowly and watched me as I did so.

A horse walked down the street below, moved sideways to avoid a bollard. A large poppy filled the window of a haberdashery.

I stretched out one arm and touched his green eyeshade. My palm, like a mucous membrane, let his face glow through it.

Is it fair, he asked me, to have given us the memory of what was and the desire of what could be when we must suffer what is?

I heard the gravel of dust in his voice, I saw smudges of graphite on his fingers. I phrased his name slowly. Morgan.

He looked up. I felt the wind of his despair. I rose slowly till my thighs were level with his face. Goodbye now, he whispered. He stepped forwards with me and opened the window. I heard it close behind me as I sank through the gloom outside.

The horse was walking slowly, his dark grace etched against the sweep of College Green. I felt tired, I had lost even the memory of desire. I sank into the poppy in the haberdasher's window. I clung to the pistil and the petals billowed round me, settling gradually into a pillow of red.

I AWOKE TO THE sounds of people. My arms were curled round that thrust of pistil with the dewdrop at the tip. The morning sun had stiffened the petals, the red pollen covered me as if their lips had bunched into a kiss. The early crowds passed by, but as I stretched my limbs groups of them gathered to stare. I drew myself upwards, bending the pistil towards me. The dewdrop fell on my face. They murmured as they watched, about portents and signs. Two soldiers pushed to the front. The pistil slipped from my hands then, I rolled down the petal and came to rest at their feet.

A man in the livery of a hotel commissionaire called on me to stand. One khaki leg prodded me, gently, but not without authority. Whom do you belong to, a voice above me asked.

I saw a small face thrusting through the thighs about me, a pair of arms full of cornheads. I gestured, but was unwilling to speak. Is he yours, the same voice asked, when he made it to my side. The boy nodded, with childlike pride and vigour. He pressed a cornhead into my hands.

I ate, and listened. You must keep him inside, one of the soldiers said, phrasing the words carefully, as one does with a child. The boy nodded, took my hand and led me forwards.

The crowd parted in front of us, but followed from behind. The commissionaire protested from amongst them. The soldier reached forward and the boy began to run. I ran too, over the grass above the paving-stones, and as the crowd followed faster, I gathered him in my arms and lost them.

We wove our way through the desultory streets. We came to a hotel with a park beside it. There was a waterless fountain there. We climbed into its stone flower and feasted on the corn-heads. Soon the petals were littered with green.

He TOLD ME he had searched for me through the depths of the building. He had waited for her, but she had never arrived. I told him I had flown, guided by a feeling that was nothing but itself. I had seen the city become a dot on the landscape and a blade of grass become a tower of green.

He told me then of Jack, who had planted a stalk that made a ladder to the skies, of how the story never told him what Jack found there. I would dearly love to fly, he said, turning his face to me. We will wait till evening, I told him, till that magic hour when our desires can picture the image that retreats from us. Will you fly to her? he asked, but I didn't reply.

All day we waited, while the sun moved the shadows through the empty grass. Some shadows walked and stopped by the fountain, gazing at us before walking on once more. He told me how the shadows thrown by the fires he stoked reminded him of the lives other boys must lead, lives he would never know anything about. Sleeping, never far from his father's calloused hands, he had longed for a friend, but could never picture what that friend might be like. A siren wailed in the distance and the city's hum rose like a final breath. What is happening? he asked, and curled his fingers round me. Nothing, I answered. Be calm.

Towards afternoon I must have slept. I imagined a moth fluttering towards the sun, the dust on its wings crackling with the heat, the flame spurring him on to his own extinction. When I awoke the mauve light had softened the shadows and given each colour a life of its own. It was evening.

The boy stood on the stone petal staring at the sky. I swung my way towards him, wrapped one arm around his torso and flew. I held his face close to mine to see the passing wonders echoed in his eyes. I bore him round at random and my desire became delight. The rush of wind drew my hair around him in a silken cloak. We flew together, out by the southern suburbs. We went far up into those realms of pure air where the rose-coloured clouds hung over the city I had loved like a brooding mushroom. The winds were fresh and keen up there. The air was aquamarine. I could see the lines of the bay very dimly, and another line too, between the metal green I knew to be the sea and the brownish mass that was the city. I sped down towards it and found not one line but two, both of which crossed at intervals, in slender figures of eight. It was the railway-track, which traced the curve of the bay. I had heard tell of these tracks, but had never yet seen them. His eyes were alert to every passing shape, as if the shadows his flaming coals threw had taken on true life. This side of the city was foreign to me, with its multitude of cramped, cracked villas tumbling towards the sea. I bore us closer to the land and found the houses gave way to a slope of trees. Though there was foliage at the tops, the trunks were quite bare and so I whipped between them, grazing the peeling bark like a swallow. The dance of those trees I apprehended without thought as I threaded my way through them and crept upwards again. We burst through the foliage and the odour there—thicker than steel wool, richer than pollen—brought to mind the one I had last held this close. I thought of musk once more. The mountainside sang of it and told me my desire had an object. The slope became a cliff, wreathed in fog. The fog bled downwards and I followed to the sea where our reflections rippled with our movement. Then there was fog no more and tracks beneath us. We passed scattered villas, imitative of a style I could not now remember. They led to a bridge, and a station beyond.

I felt the panic of a desire that had led me truly. I traced a large arc over the eaves of the station. There was a line of pleasure-parlours by a crumbling promenade. In one of them a yellow light glimmered.

SHE WAS STANDING by the dodgems in a blue smock. There were blotches on her face and runnels of hair along her arms. The changes, she told me, were so rapid that each day was a source of sometimes wonder, sometimes terror, sometimes both. She had longed to see me, but had been unwilling to approach, since she felt the need of a partner to delight in them. Could you now? she asked, and came towards me, the pits and shallows of her face raised in expectation. Yes, I said, but the word that emerged did not seem affirmative. So, she said, I must find another. She brushed my translucent face with her bunched fingers. Business was even worse, she told me, in the realms of entertainment than in the realm of perfume. Her friends had shunned her, she told me, seeing her as a sign, of a happening they would never allude to or define. And yet I am glad, she said. Tell me why I am glad. The fact, I told her, is a relief from its anticipation. And the feeling is all. She drew her swollen lips into a smile. Once more, she understood. A soldier entered then, his head bent low, his hands thrust deep into his khakis. You must leave now, she whispered. She drew her smock around her face and walked towards him.

We slipped through the shadows, the boy and I. I drew him over the awning in one sad curve. The soldier parted her tresses below us. She sighed with anticipated pleasure. We hovered above them, like uninvited guests, until I drew him towards the sea once more.

THE WATERS were calm, a long shallow pit of salt. All hint of reflection had now vanished. They were graced by a thin pall of mist.

You cannot blame her, the boy said. His voice bounced over the waters.

No, I replied. I sank with him to just above that mist.

She loved you, he said. But only for a time.

His wisdom was comforting. I fell with him into the sea and held him there, buoyed by an excess of salt.

He remarked on how it tasted like tears. I agreed with him. We let the sea carry us, and the night.

WHEN DAY came up, we saw that the city with its crumbling cubes was far behind us. The waters steamed gently. The liquid rose in a diaphanous haze and left behind pure crystals of salt. They stayed poised beneath the surface like a thousand eyes. I twined myself into a vessel beneath him and moved us forwards with my broad fingers. He told me of the mermaid who had ventured on land and to whom each footstep was like the thrust of a blade. Soon my arms became covered in a crystal sheen.

The sun moved slowly on the waters. At its pinnacle the haze was such that it multiplied itself. I swam on. The boy wondered whether the sun moved backwards out here. But no, it was merely the illusion of haze.

I felt little need to speak. The sound of the water, oddly reverberant in the ever-present vapour, made speech enough. The boy talked as the spirit moved him. He had strands of my hair wrapped around his fists, in excitement or anticipation. Then night came down and the light gave way quite unobtrusively.

WE MUST HAVE slept, for I awoke to moonlight and a sense of turbulence. The sea all about us was calm, however, and the moon was brilliant in the absence of haze. The boy still slept. I heard a prodding all around me which merged into a voice. I saw Alarth winging towards me across the waters. Come, come, he whispered. A winged fish broke the surface, twisted silver under the moonlight and enveloped him in its maw. Then a white flash filled the air from the city we had left. It was paler than any white that had been and was followed by others, each paler again till the white seemed permanent. Then the sounds came, all the sounds at once, from the deepest to the thinnest in a circular boom, they sang towards us in waves, and hard on their heels the waters followed. I covered the boy and was dragged by the mountain of water.

WHAT CAME WAS not quite daylight and not quite night. The waters were calm and strewn with debris and cut grass. I had twined myself into a pouch round the boy. Far behind us that cloud, shaped like a phoenix, glowed with that terrible mauve. I stroked my fingers and moved us towards a promontory beyond.

A marble arm lay on the whitened sand. The boy was sick, I knew. His translucent lips tried to speak, but couldn't. I rose with him from the waters and made my way across that sand. There were the marks of feet. A fish twined its way round a clump of seagrass, its gills moving easily. I followed the webbed footprints.

When the time came that I knew the boy was dying, I wrapped myself fully round him, assumed him into myself. We both walked onwards, though my steps were weary with the knowledge that I would never see his face again. I remembered the cornheads, but felt no need for food. After a time those footprints were joined by others.

Each knew where to go, with no need of direction. With the mareotic sea far behind me, I took their advice. Many, many footprints later I came to a pool. The boy in me drew me to its surface. I put my lips to it and drank and felt his satisfaction. When the rippling caused by my lips had settled, I saw a reflection there, no less terrible than mine. A hand rubbed white sand away from a mouth. It was like mine in its shape and texture. Her hair, unmistakably female, was a whey-coloured fan in the constant wind. I raised my head and the boy inside me leapt. Her lips moved slowly and creased themselves upwards. My lips moved too. I recognised Marianne.

WE SPOKE for a while, by the pool. Once accustomed to each other's voices, we both walked together, following the footprints before us. We had similar memories of the mareotic lake. She told me of a fish that walked and of a tree that shed its covering of scales. Matilde, she told me, was inside her now. I put my arms down to her waist and felt her. The boy kicked with pleasure at the touch.

Once a large beast flew above us and her hand gripped mine. We followed the footprints, but met no others. Soon the sands gave way to a vista of grass. The labour of our feet was lessened then, that soft cushion drew us onwards. The footprints had ceased, but we followed our own path. We crossed a hill and found a landscape of tall poplars. Planted years ago, it seemed to speak of quieter times. If things lead us to anything, she said to me, they surely lead us to realisation. Each happening bears a message, as surely as those poplars speak of whoever planted them. She curled her fingers round my hand once more and I saw the translucence was slowly fading, being replaced by something like a tan. The line of poplars led us to a signpost reading: HOPE ETERNAL. The arrow had wound itself into a circle, though, the point of which pressed into its rear. There was a garden up ahead. The gates were unattended and the grasses wild. The sundial seemed bleached by an eternity of light and the sprinklers moved so slowly that they whispered. Can I kiss you, she asked and I answered yes, in a voice that had become like hers. She had to tilt her head to reach my lips which I found were once more soft. The kiss was long, long enough for the sun to cross the dial, for the moon to traverse it and for the sun to rise once more. I saw the globes of her eyes and in my visage reflected there saw something as human as surprise.

The

Crying

Game

an original screenplay

CHARACTERS

(in order of appearance)

JODY
JUDE
FERGUS HENNESSY
PETER MAGUIRE
TINKER
TOMMY
DIL
COL
DAVE
TRISTRAM DEVEROUX
FRANKNUM

EXTERIOR. CARNIVAL—DAY.

A loudspeaker playing Percy Sledge's "When a Man Loves a Woman," as we see a carnival in the distance—with a Ferris Wheel turning round and round.

A black man is by a stall. On his arm is an Irish girl with blond hair. The black man is drunk, and is tossing rings around a bowling pin.

JODY: And that's cricket, hon.

An attendant hands him the teddy bear. It looks ridiculous in his huge hands. He gives it to the girl.

JODY: You want it?

GIRL: Sure.

JODY: Doesn't matter if you don't.

He puts his arm around her and drags her on.

JODY: Jody won't be offended. Jody's never offended. What'd you say your name was?

GIRL: Jude.

JODY: Jude. Suits you, Jude.

JUDE: The teddy bear?

JODY: No, fuck the bear. The name. Jude. And it's June. Jude in June.

He comes to a small canvas tent with a sign on it—TOILET.

JODY: Gotta piss, Jude.

He holds her hand.

JODY: Don't run off, Jude.

JUDE: You don't know me, do you?

Jody walks inside the canvas flap and vanishes from sight. We can still see his hand, holding Jude's. She leans against the canvas, looking bored.

JODY *(inside)*: What if I did?

JUDE: You'd know I wouldn't run off.

She stands there, listening to the sound of him urinate. Her eyes flick around the carnival. They settle on a tall dark-haired man in a dark jacket. He nods.

JODY: Never pissed holding a girl's hand, Jude.

JUDE: You didn't?

JODY: And you know what?

JUDE: Tell me, Jody.

He staggers out, buttoning up.

JODY: It's nice.

He goes to kiss her. She turns her head away.

JUDE: Not here.

JODY: Who gives a fuck.

JUDE: You never know.

She pulls him over toward the water.

JODY: I never know nothing.

JUDE: People. They could be looking.

Jody follows her, as she walks backward, drawing him on. He moves his hips to a song as Jude leads him over the beach, under a train trestle.

JUDE: Come and get me, soldier—

JODY: Whatever you say, Jude . . .

He sinks down on his knees toward her. She wraps her arms around his neck and kisses him. Jody writhes on top of her, fumbling with his belt. Jude cocks one eye upward. A shadow falls across them.

CLOSE ON JODY, *kissing her. A gun is put to his head. He turns around, drunkenly.*

JODY: What the fuck—

The gun whacks him across the cheek and he falls sideways.

Jude scrambles to her feet and darts like an animal through a field.

Jody feels his cheek. He can see her blond head vanishing among the fields. He looks up and sees a group of men around him. The tallest of them, Fergus, cocks the gun.

INTERIOR. CAR—DAY.

A mini, driving down a country road. Two men in the front, three in the back.

On the floor of the car Jody lies, with three pairs of feet on top of him, a black bag over his head and the barrel of a gun dangling close to his face. Fergus holds the gun. He is smoking a cigarette. His movements are slow and somewhat innocent.

FERGUS: So what's your name, soldier?

JODY: Fuck you.

FERGUS: Yeah.

EXTERIOR. SMALL FARMHOUSE—EVENING.

INTERIOR. FARMHOUSE—NIGHT.

Jody pulled through and tied to a chair. Maguire, a small lean man, talks to him through the hood.

MAGUIRE: The situation is simple. You're being held hostage by the Irish Republican Army. They've got one of our senior members under interrogation in Castleraigh. We've informed them that if they don't release him within three days, you'll be shot. You'll be treated as our guest until further developments. Have you anything to say?

Jody is motionless under the black hood.

FERGUS: Give him a cup of tea.

MAGUIRE: Do you want a cup of tea?

He still says nothing.

DISSOLVE.

All the men are drinking tea. The blond woman comes in with a plate and some food on it.

FERGUS: See does he want some.

JUDE: Do you want some food?

Jody sits as still as a grave, saying nothing.

DISSOLVE.

Late at night—it is dark. The men are sleeping. Fergus is sitting by a chair, gun in his hand, watching the prisoner. Jude comes in, with a flashlight.

FERGUS: Hey—what's he like?

JUDE: Horny bastard.

FERGUS: Did you give him it?

JUDE: There are certain things I wouldn't do for my country.

FERGUS: Have a look at him.

JUDE: Can't.

FERGUS: Poke him or something. See if he's still alive.

JUDE: He's all right.

FERGUS: Hasn't moved for twelve hours. Go on. Have a heart.

She moves over to him. She prods him in the legs with her foot. He doesn't move. Then she lifts the hood ever so slightly, to peer inside. Suddenly the man moves like lightning, jerking his head down so the hood comes off, throwing his body, tied to the chair, over Jude.

JODY: You fucking bitch—you fucking whore—

He pins her to the ground, his body bent with the chair. He writhes on top of her in a grotesque parody of love. She is screaming and the room is alive, each man awake, grabbing guns, screaming.

MAGUIRE: Turn the fucking thing off—

EXTERIOR. FARMHOUSE—NIGHT.

Fergus follows Jude out a back door, holding her by the arm.

FERGUS: You all right?

JUDE: Fucking animal.

She takes in huge gobs of air.

FERGUS: You don't know that.

JUDE: Fucking do. I had him all over me.

He touches her face.

FERGUS: Tough work, that.

JUDE: Someone's got to do it.

She rubs her hand on his chest.

JUDE: Nah, it was a breeze. Just thought of you.

She sidles closer, coming on to him.

JUDE: And you know what, Fergus? One of you made me want it . . .

She puts her lips to his neck.

FERGUS: Which one?

She doesn't answer. They embrace.

EXTERIOR. FARMHOUSE—MORNING.

A hot summer's day. There are tall hedges all around the house. Fergus leads Jody, still bound and hooded, over toward a greenhouse.

INTERIOR. GREENHOUSE—DAY.

Dusty tomato plants and vines everywhere. Broken glass. The sun pouring through. Fergus leads Jody over to a wrought iron chair and sits him in it. He sits opposite, gun on his lap. Fergus takes some sandwiches out of a brown paper bag. He holds one out toward him.

FERGUS: Eat something, would you?

JODY: Can't.

FERGUS: What do you mean you can't?

JODY: Can't eat through a canvas bag.

Fergus walks over to him, lifts the hood up so his mouth is revealed, and pushes the sandwich toward his lips. Jody eats, slowly.

JODY: This is a farce, man.

FERGUS: How is it a farce?

JODY: I seen your fucking face.

FERGUS: So, what do I look like?

JODY: You're the one about five ten with the killer smile and the baby face.

FERGUS: Am I?

JODY: Yeah. And the brown eyes.

Fergus pushes the last crumbs of the sandwich toward Jody's mouth.

JODY: You're the handsome one.

Jody eats the last bits.

JODY: Thank you, handsome.

FERGUS: My pleasure.

EXTERIOR. FARMHOUSE—DAY.

Jude makes her way from the door toward the greenhouse. She is carrying a pot of tea and two cups.

INTERIOR. GREENHOUSE—DAY.

It is sweltering now in the greenhouse. CLOSE ON JODY'S COWLED HEAD. The hood is drenched with sweat.

JODY: I can't fucking breathe, man. Be a Christian, will you?

Jude comes into view.

JODY: Tell him to take the hood off, honey . . .

Jude says nothing. Lays the tea on the ground.

FERGUS: How did you know it was her?

JODY: I can smell her perfume.

Jude pours out the tea.

JUDE: See, if we took the hood off, we'd have to shoot you. As it is, you've got a fifty-fifty chance.

JODY: Thought you liked me, bitch.

JUDE: It was fun while it lasted.

JODY: Nice lady.

His breathing becomes labored.

JODY: Please, man, I'm suffocating in here.

FERGUS: Can't we take it off?

JUDE: Have to check with himself.

Fergus gives her the gun.

FERGUS: You look after him.

Jody's head follows Fergus while he leaves.

JODY: Don't leave me with her, man. She's dangerous . . .

Jude smiles, holding the gun on her lap.

INTERIOR. FARMHOUSE—DAY.

Fergus enters. Maguire and the others. Maguire has a newspaper, which has a headline regarding the kidnapping.

MAGUIRE: Made the front page. They'll move now, the fuckers.

FERGUS: Request permission to take the hood off, Tommy.

MAGUIRE: Why would you do that?

FERGUS: The poor whore's suffocating in the heat.

MAGUIRE: So?

FERGUS: And anyway, he's seen our faces.

MAGUIRE: You sure?

FERGUS: He described me down to a T. Knows what Jude looks like.

Maguire reads the paper.

FERGUS: Tommy—

MAGUIRE: You're his keeper. If you don't mind him seeing you, I don't mind. But you're the only one he looks at.

FERGUS: Thanks.

MAGUIRE: It's your decision.

INTERIOR. GREENHOUSE—DAY.

Jude, drinking tea, looking at Jody sweating. Fergus enters. He puts his arm casually around her.

FERGUS: Leave us, Judie.

JUDE: My pleasure.

She goes. Fergus walks to Jody and slowly takes the hood off. Jody looks up at him, his face bathed in sweat. He breathes in mighty gulps of air. He smiles.

JODY: Thank you, soldier.

Fergus smiles.

JODY: Never thought fresh air would taste this good.

Fergus pours out a cup of tea and brings it to his lips.

JODY: Now, if you took the ropes off, I'd be able to feed myself.

FERGUS: No fucking way.

JODY: Only joking.

Fergus drinks.

JODY: You know, I was wrong about one thing.

FERGUS: What's that?

JODY: Five ten. Brown eyes. But you're no pinup.

FERGUS: No?

JODY: Nope. Not handsome at all.

FERGUS: You trying to hurt my feelings?

JODY: No. It's the truth.

FERGUS: Well, I could say the same about you.

JODY: Could you?

FERGUS: But I won't. We're more polite around these parts.

JODY: So I've noticed.

Fergus looks at him. Jody isn't smiling anymore. Fergus goes back to his seat and drinks his tea. He fingers the gun on his lap.

JODY: Hey—

FERGUS: What is it now?

JODY: You're going to have to do it, aren't you?

FERGUS: Do what?

JODY: Kill me.

FERGUS: What makes you think that?

JODY: They're going to let that guy die. And you're going to kill me.

FERGUS: They won't let him die.

JODY: You want to bet?

FERGUS: I'm not a gambling man.

JODY: And even if he doesn't die—you can't just let me loose.

FERGUS: Why can't we?

JODY: Not in your nature.

FERGUS: What do you know about my nature?

JODY: I'm talking about your people, not you.

FERGUS: What the fuck do you know about my people?

JODY: Only that you're all tough undeluded motherfuckers. And that it's not in your nature to let me go.

FERGUS: Shut the fuck up, would you?

JODY: And you know the funny thing?

FERGUS: No, what's the funny thing?

JODY: I didn't even fancy her.

FERGUS: Didn't look like that to me . . .

JODY: She's not my type.

He looks at Fergus.

JODY: C'mere.

FERGUS: No.

JODY: Ah, c'mere. I want to show you something.

FERGUS: What?

JODY: My inside pocket.

Fergus holds the gun to his face. He fishes inside Jody's inside pocket.

JODY: Take out the wallet.

Fergus's hand emerges with a wallet.

JODY: Open it.

CLOSE ON THE WALLET. *Credit cards, army identification photograph.*

JODY: Inside. There's a picture.

Fergus takes out a picture. It is of Jody, in cricket whites, smiling, holding a bat. Fergus smiles.

JODY: No, not that one. There's another.

Fergus takes out another picture of Jody and of a beautiful black woman, smiling.

JODY: Now *she's* my type.

FERGUS: She'd be anyone's type.

JODY: Don't you think of it, fucker.

FERGUS: Why not?

JODY: She's mine. Anyway, she wouldn't suit you.

FERGUS: No?

JODY: Absolutely not.

FERGUS: She your wife?

JODY: Suppose you could say that.

Jody chuckles.

FERGUS: You make a nice couple.

JODY: Don't I know it.

FERGUS: So what were you fucking around for, then?

JODY: You fuckers set me up. That bitch—

FERGUS: She's a friend of mine—

JODY: Okay. That nice lady. Meets me in a bar. I'm saying what the fuck am I doing here anyway. She buys me a drink. She holds my hand. I'm looking at her saying I don't like you, bitch. But what the fuck. Maybe I'll get to understand.

FERGUS: What?

JODY: What the fuck am I doing here.

FERGUS: What the fuck were you doing here?

JODY: I got sent.

FERGUS: You could have said no.

JODY: Can't. Once I signed up.

FERGUS: Why did you sign up?

JODY: It was a job. So I get sent to the only place in the world they call you nigger to your face.

FERGUS: Shouldn't take it personally.

JODY (*He imitates a Belfast accent*): "Go back to your banana tree, nigger." No use telling them I came from Tottenham.

FERGUS: And you play cricket?

JODY: Best game in the world.

FERGUS: Ever see hurling?

JODY: That game where a bunch of paddies whack sticks at each other?

FERGUS: Best game in the world.

JODY: Never.

FERGUS: The fastest.

JODY: Well, in Antigua cricket's the black man's game. The kids play it from the age of two. My daddy had me throwing googlies from the age of five. Then we moved to Tottenham and it was something different.

FERGUS: How different?

JODY: Toffs' game there. But not at home.

Fergus looks at him.

JODY: So when you come to shoot me, Paddy, remember, you're getting rid of a shit-hot bowler.

FERGUS: I'll bear that in mind.

He keeps looking at him.

FERGUS: And by the way, it's not Paddy. It's Fergus.

Jody smiles.

JODY: Nice to meet you, Fergus.

FERGUS: My pleasure, Jody.

EXTERIOR. GREENHOUSE—NIGHT.

Fergus leads Jody outside, holding the gun against him.

FERGUS: Take it easy, now. Just go slow. Down by that tree.

JODY: Tree.

He walks toward it, breathing heavily.

JODY: You've got to loosen my hands.

FERGUS: Can't.

JODY: Well then, you're going to have to take my dick out for me, aren't you?

Fergus, in the dark, stands motionless, looking at him.

JODY: Come on, man, I'm going to wet my pants!

Fergus turns him around and unzips his fly.

JODY: Take the fucker out, man, I'm dying—

Fergus takes Jody's penis out.

Jody takes two steps toward the wall.

JODY: I gotta lean forward or I'll dribble all over myself. Will you hold my hands for me.

*Fergus holds his hands from behind, so Jody can lean forward.
Jody now pisses with immense relief.*

JODY: Now, that was worth waiting for.

FERGUS: Hurry up, would you?

JODY: These things take time, Fergus.

He shakes his body.

JODY: It's amazing how these small details take on such importance . . .

He steps back.

JODY: Now put it back in.

FERGUS: Give us a break.

JODY: I can't do it! It's only a piece of meat. For fuck's sake, it's
got no major diseases.

Fergus puts Jody's penis back in his pants and zips him up.

JODY: Thank you. I had a case of the clap two years ago. Crabs
in Ulster. But all in all it's served me well.

FERGUS: Shut up, would you?

JODY: I'm sorry. Didn't mean to offend you, Fergus.

Fergus leads him back toward the greenhouse.

INTERIOR. GREENHOUSE—NIGHT.

Fergus leads Jody back to his chair.

JODY: Fergus?

FERGUS: Yeah?

JODY: Thanks. I know that wasn't easy for you.

He begins to laugh.

FERGUS: The pleasure was all mine.

Fergus begins to laugh, without knowing why.

EXTERIOR. FARMHOUSE—NIGHT.

Maguire, walking out of the house, woken by the sound of laughter.

INTERIOR. GREENHOUSE—NIGHT.

Jody, still laughing. Suddenly the hood is slammed back over his head.

Maguire, standing there in the dark, looking at Fergus.

MAGUIRE: What the fuck is this?

FERGUS: It's nothing. He's just got a sense of humor, that's all.

MAGUIRE: You're on duty. Keep your fucking mouth shut. Go in and get some sleep.

Fergus gets up slowly, walks toward the door.

JODY: Yeah. Get some sleep.

EXTERIOR. FARMHOUSE—NIGHT.

Fergus, walking toward the house. He looks back and sees the figures of Maguire and Jody, in the dark, in absolute silence.

INTERIOR. FARMHOUSE—NIGHT.

Fergus sleeping.

INTERIOR. GREENHOUSE—NIGHT.

Jody sleeping. Maguire sitting with an Armalite in his hands, watching him.

EXTERIOR. FARMHOUSE AND FIELDS—DAY.

The sun coming up over the low hills around the farmhouse.

INTERIOR. GREENHOUSE—DAY.

Fergus enters, with a tray and some breakfast. Maguire is sitting where he sat before, stock-still.

FERGUS: Did he talk?

Maguire shakes his head.

FERGUS: Didn't make you laugh?

Maguire shakes his head.

FERGUS: Here. Have some breakfast.

He hands Maguire a plate. Jody stirs.

JODY: Good morning, Fergus?

Maguire looks hard at him.

MAGUIRE: So he knows your name?

FERGUS: I told him.

MAGUIRE: Are you all there?

He rises, and drags Fergus out the door.

FERGUS: Back in a minute, Jody.

EXTERIOR. GREENHOUSE—DAY.

MAGUIRE: You'll have minimal contact with the prisoner, do you
    hear me?

FERGUS: Yes.

MAGUIRE: And do you know why?

FERGUS: Why?

MAGUIRE: Because tomorrow we might have to shoot him, that's
    why.

Maguire goes back to the house.

INTERIOR. GREENHOUSE—DAY.

Jody sitting with the hood on again. Fergus enters.

JODY: They giving you trouble, Fergus?

Fergus says nothing. He takes a plate and brings it toward Jody.

JODY: It happens. Y'see, there's two kinds of people. Those who give and those who take.

Fergus lifts up Jody's hood to expose his mouth and begins to feed him.

JODY: Ah, take the thing off, man.

Fergus says nothing and keeps feeding him.

JODY: It's okay. I understand. Don't mind if I prattle on, do you?

Fergus shakes his head and says nothing.

JODY: I will take it by your silence that you don't.

He eats. Fergus feeds himself, then feeds more to Jody.

JODY: Two types, Fergus. The scorpion and the frog. Ever heard of them?

Fergus says nothing.

JODY: Scorpion wants to cross a river, but he can't swim. Goes to the frog, who can, and asks for a ride. Frog says, "If I give you a ride on my back, you'll go and sting me." Scorpion replies, "It would not be in my interest to sting you since as I'll be on your back we both would drown." Frog thinks about this logic for a while and accepts the deal. Takes the scorpion on his back. Braves the waters. Halfway over feels a burning spear in his side and realizes the scorpion has stung him after all. And as they both sink beneath the waves the frog cries out, "Why did you sting me, Mr Scorpion, for now we both will drown?" Scorpion replies, "I can't help it, it's in my nature."

Jody chuckles under his hood.

FERGUS: So what's that supposed to mean?

JODY: Means what it says. The scorpion does what is in his nature. Take off the hood, man.

FERGUS: Why?

JODY: 'Cause you're kind. It's in your nature.

Fergus walks toward him and pulls off the hood. Jody smiles up at him.

JODY: See? I was right about you.

FERGUS: Don't be so sure.

JODY: Jody's always right.

INTERIOR. GREENHOUSE—LATE AFTERNOON.

Both men dozing in the heat.

JODY: Where would you most like to be now, man?

FERGUS: Doesn't matter where.

JODY: Come on, man. If this shit was all over.

FERGUS: Having a pint in the Rock.

JODY: You lack imagination, Fergus. Think of something more alluring.

FERGUS: Like what?

JODY: Like having a pint in the Metro—

Fergus laughs.

FERGUS: Having two pints in the Rock.

JODY: Having a pint in the Metro, and Dil's having a margarita.

FERGUS: Who's Dil?

JODY: My special friend.

FERGUS: Oh, yeah.

JODY: We got simple tastes, you and me.

FERGUS: The best.

JODY: But you fellas never get a break, do you?

FERGUS: Do you?

JODY: Oh, yes. We do a tour of duty and we're finished. But you guys are never finished, are you?

FERGUS: We don't look on it like that.

JODY: I've often wondered how you do it.

FERGUS: Depends on what you believe in.

JODY: What do you believe in?

FERGUS: That you guys shouldn't be here.

JODY: It's as simple as that?

FERGUS: Yes.

Jude enters.

JUDE: Put that thing back on him, Fergus.

FERGUS: He's hot.

JUDE: Doesn't matter if he's hot. Just cover the fucker up.

JODY: Have you no feelings, woman?

JUDE: You shut your face—

She pulls the hood down over him.

JUDE: You're heading for trouble, Fergus—

JODY: He's a good soldier, Jude.

She whacks him with a pistol.

JUDE: I said shut the fuck up—

JODY: He believes in the future—

INTERIOR. GREENHOUSE—NIGHT.

Jody, sitting in the hood. Fergus lifts it a bit; Jody's mouth, with blood now in his lips.

FERGUS: Is it bad?

JODY: No. Not bad. Women are trouble, you know that, Fergus?

FERGUS: I didn't.

JODY: Some kinds of women are . . .

FERGUS: She can't help it.

JODY: Dil wasn't trouble. No trouble at all.

FERGUS: You liked her?

JODY: Present tense, please. Love her. Whatever she is. I'm thinking of her now, Fergus. Will you think of her too?

FERGUS: Don't know her.

JODY: Want you to do something, Fergus.

FERGUS: What?

JODY: If they kill me—

FERGUS: Don't think that way.

JODY: But they will. As sure as night follows day. They have to. I want you to find her out. Tell her I was thinking of her.

Fergus is moved. He can't reply.

JODY: See if she's all right.

FERGUS: I don't know her.

JODY: Take her picture. C'mere.

Fergus walks toward him.

JODY: Take it. In the inside pocket.

Their faces, close to each other as Fergus searches out her picture.

JODY: Take the whole lot. I won't need it.

FERGUS: I told you not to talk that way—

JODY: Go to Millie's Hair Salon in Spitalfields. Take her to the Metro for a margarita. Don't have to tell her who you are. Just tell her Jody was thinking—

FERGUS: Stop it—

The door opens. Maguire is there, with another.

MAGUIRE: Volunteer?

Fergus turns toward him.

MAGUIRE: We need you inside.

Fergus walks toward Maguire and the other man walks forward, takes his seat. Fergus, unseen by Maguire, puts the wallet in his pocket.

INTERIOR. FARMHOUSE—NIGHT.

Maguire, Jude, Fergus, and the others.

MAGUIRE: We've had word. They've used every trick in the book on him. He's starting to talk. You're going to have to do it in the morning.

Maguire lights a cigarette. Fergus looks at him and nods.

MAGUIRE: You OK about that?

FERGUS: I'm a volunteer, am n't I?

MAGUIRE: Good. I was beginning to have my doubts about you for the last few days.

JUDE: Not the only one—

MAGUIRE: Shut up, Jude. You best get some sleep tonight, Fergus.

FERGUS: Peter.

MAGUIRE: What?

FERGUS: Request permission to guard the prisoner tonight—

JUDE: You're crazy. Don't let him, Peter.

MAGUIRE: Shut the fuck up, Jude.

He turns back to Fergus. He puts his arm on Fergus's shoulder.

MAGUIRE: Why do you want to do that for?

FERGUS: Would make me feel better about it.

MAGUIRE: You sure about that?

FERGUS: I'm sure.

MAGUIRE: Okay. You're a good man, Fergus.

Fergus leaves.

INTERIOR. GREENHOUSE—NIGHT.

Fergus takes his place in the chair beside Jody.

Jody begins to laugh under the hood. It turns into the sound of crying.

FERGUS: Don't.

JODY: I'm sorry.

The crying stops.

JODY: Help me.

FERGUS: How can I?

JODY: I don't know. Just help me. Give me a cigarette.

Fergus takes out a cigarette, lights it, and lifts up Jody's hood so he can smoke.

JODY: Don't even smoke, you know that? It just seemed the right thing to do.

Fergus watches him puff the cigarette, the hood just above his lips. Jody coughs, but keeps the cigarette in his lips. Fergus gently takes the cigarette from his mouth.

FERGUS: Go to sleep now.

JODY: I don't want to sleep. Tell me something.

FERGUS: What?

JODY: A story.

FERGUS: Like the one about the frog?

JODY: And the scorpion. No. Tell me anything.

FERGUS: When I was a child . . .

JODY: Yeah?

FERGUS: I thought as a child. But when I became a man I put away childish things . . .

JODY: What does that mean?

FERGUS: Nothing.

JODY: Tell me something, anything.

Fergus is silent; his eyes wet.

JODY: Not a lot of use, are you, Fergus?

FERGUS: Me? No, I'm not good for much . . .

EXTERIOR. FIELDS—MORNING.

The farmhouse covered in mist. The sun coming through it.

EXTERIOR. GREENHOUSE—MORNING.

Maguire opens the door to the greenhouse and clicks the chamber of his gun. Fergus has a gun in his hand. He checks the chamber.

Fergus takes Jody, whose hands are still tied behind his back, by the elbow.

FERGUS: Stand up, now—

Jody rises. Fergus leads him through the door, past Maguire.

MAGUIRE: I wish to say on behalf of the Irish Republican Army—

Fergus turns with sudden fierceness.

FERGUS: Leave him be—

He pulls Jody through the fields.

EXTERIOR. TREES—MORNING.

Fergus pushing Jody through a copse of trees, the gun at his back.

JODY: Take the hood off, Fergus—

FERGUS: No.

JODY: I want to see a bit. Please, please. Don't make me die like an animal.

Fergus pulls the hood off. Jody looks around him. He has a cut lip where Jude struck him.

Fergus prods him on with the gun. Jody stumbles forward. Fergus is all cold and businesslike.

JODY: I'm glad you're doing it, do you know that, Fergus?

FERGUS: Why?

JODY: 'Cause you're my friend. And I want you to go to the Metro—

FERGUS: Stop that talk now—

JODY: Hurling's a fast game, isn't it, Fergus?

FERGUS: The fastest.

JODY: Faster than cricket?

FERGUS: Cricket's in the halfpenny place.

JODY: So if I ran now, there's no way I'd beat you, is there?

FERGUS: You won't run.

JODY: But if I did . . . you wouldn't shoot a brother in the back—

Jody suddenly sprints, and, loosening the ties on his hands, then freeing them, he is off like a hare. Fergus screams in fury after him.

FERGUS: JODY!!!

Fergus aims, then changes his mind and runs.

FERGUS: You stupid bastard—

JODY: What you say, faster?

FERGUS: I said you bastard—stop—

JODY: Got to catch me first—

Fergus gains on him—stretches his arm out—but Jody sprints ahead again—as if he has been playing with him. He laughs in exhilaration. Fergus pants behind him, wheezing, almost laughing.

JODY: Used to run the mile, you know—four times round the cricket pitch—what was that game called?

FERGUS: Hurling—

JODY: What?

FERGUS: Hurling—

Jody runs, whipping through the trees—always ahead of him.

JODY: Come on, Fergie—you can do it—a bit more wind—

Fergus grabs his shoulder and Jody shrugs it off, gaining on him again.

JODY: Bit of fun, Fergus, eh?

And suddenly the trees give way. Jody turns, laughing, to Fergus.

JODY: Told you I was fast—

Fergus is panting, pointing the gun at Jody.

JODY: Don't do it.

And suddenly a Saracen tank whips around the corner, hits Jody with the full of its fender. His body flies in the air and bounces forward as another tank tries to grind to a halt and the huge wheels grind over him.

Fergus, screaming, "No—!" He almost moves forward, then sees soldiers spilling from the tank around the body. Fergus turns and runs.

EXTERIOR. TREES—DAY.

Fergus whipping through the trees, his body crouched low as he runs.

INTERIOR. GREENHOUSE—DAY.

Tinker sitting in the greenhouse. A helicopter screams into view through the panes and automatic fire comes from it, shattering every pane in seconds and tearing Tinker to bits.

INTERIOR. FARMHOUSE—DAY.

Bullets whipping through every window, taking chunks from the masonry, tearing the walls apart. Maguire, Jude, and the others on the floor, scrambling for weapons.

EXTERIOR. TREES—DAY.

Fergus, hearing the gunfire, runs through overhanging branches till eventually he is hidden from sight.

EXTERIOR. CARNIVAL ON THE MONAGHAN BORDER—DAWN.

A forlorn-looking building over nondescript fields.

An old man wheels a bicycle slowly toward it; a rusty car appears; and Fergus gets out of it.

TOMMY: Fergus!

FERGUS: You're back in the pink, Tommy? How're you keeping?

INTERIOR. CARAVAN—DAY.

The old man pouring whiskey into a teacup.

TOMMY: You'll notice I've asked you nothing.

FERGUS: That's wise, Tommy.

TOMMY: All right, then. I like to be wise.

He pours Fergus more whiskey.

TOMMY: So what do you need, Fergus?

FERGUS: Need to go across the water.

TOMMY: Do you now.

FERGUS: Need to lose myself awhile.

TOMMY: Aha.

He looks at Fergus and lights a cigarette.

He puffs.

TOMMY: There's a man I know ships cattle to London.

EXTERIOR. DUBLIN BAY—EVENING.

The ferry, churning into the sunset.

FADE TO BLACK.

INTERIOR. BUILDING SITE—DAY.

FADE UP into an elegant, empty Georgian room, covered in clouds of dust. A figure among the clouds of dust, hacking at a wall with a sledgehammer. It is Fergus, dressed in laborer's overalls, covered in dust. He is knocking the bricks from an outer wall. He works furiously and relentlessly, like a machine.

We see the wall, with the hammer striking it. One brick falls away, then another. Daylight pours through the clouds of dust and the growing hole.

Fergus's face, as he works.

The hole. More bricks falling away. Through the clouds of dust and the streams of daylight we now see a patch of green.

Fergus's face, working. His rhythm slows.

The hole. More bricks fall away. Then the hammer stops. The dust begins to clear.

His face.

The jagged hole. The dust drifts across it, revealing a cricket pitch, with tiny sticklike figures running on the green.

EXTERIOR. HOSTEL—DAY.

Fergus, returning from work, crosses the street, and enters through a white door.

INTERIOR. HOSTEL—DAY.

Fergus dressing. He puts on a cheap suit, like any country boy in a big city. He takes Jody's wallet from the trousers of his overalls. He flips it open, sees the picture of the soldier and Dil. He puts it in the pocket of his suit.

EXTERIOR. STREET—DAY.

Fergus walking down a street looking for an address. Some distance down the street is a sign—MILLIE'S UNISEX HAIR SALON.

EXTERIOR. STREET—DAY.

Fergus, standing as the crowds go by him, looking in the window. He has the picture in his hand. We see Dil from his point of view, then Fergus walks inside.

INTERIOR. HAIR SALON—DAY.

Fergus enters. The door gives a loud ping.

A GIRL: We're closing. I'll see you tomorrow, Dil.

She leaves the salon.

DIL: You want something in particular?

FERGUS: Just a bit of a trim . . .

Dil checks her watch and stubs out a cigarette.

DIL: Come on . . .

She gestures toward a chair. Fergus sits down. She comes toward him and fiddles with his hair.

She pushes his head back into a basin behind him. She begins to knead his hair in hot water and shampoo.

DIL: Someone recommend you?

FERGUS: In a way.

DIL: Who?

FERGUS: Guy I work with.

DIL: What's his name?

Fergus can't think of an answer. The hands with the purple nails run over his scalp.

FERGUS: Doesn't the water get to your nails?

DIL: What's it to you?

FERGUS: Nothing.

Fergus, sitting up. She begins to cut.

DIL: You American?

FERGUS: No.

DIL: Not English.

FERGUS: No.

DIL: Scottish?

FERGUS: How'd you guess?

DIL: The accent, I suppose.

FERGUS: And what's it like?

DIL: Like treacle.

She imitates his accent saying it. Fergus laughs.

DIL: Nice laugh.

Dil raises Fergus's head up, with his new-cut hair and holds a mirror up behind his head so he can see the back. He looks like a young London stockbroker. The hair salon around them is empty.

DIL: That should make her happy.

FERGUS: Who's she?

DIL: Don't know. Who is she?

EXTERIOR. HAIR SALON—EVENING.

Fergus emerges from the shop. He takes one last look through the window where Dil is taking off her smock, touching up her hair, etc. It is as if she has forgotten all about him. He walks off through the crowds and then ducks into a doorway.

The doorway of the shop. Dil comes out, dressed in a pair of high heels, a very short skirt, different, more raunchy clothes on her than we saw inside. She locks the glass door and walks down the street, across the road, and into a pub called the Metro. Fergus follows.

INTERIOR. METRO—EVENING.

Half full, with an after-work crowd. Dil makes her way through it.

BARMAN: Hi, Dil.

DIL: Hiya, hon.

She sits down at the bar. Fergus comes toward the bar and takes a seat.

BARMAN: What'll it be?

FERGUS: A bottle of Guinness.

Dil, looking at Fergus.

DIL: See that, Col?

COL: See what, Dil?

DIL: He gave me a look.

COL: Did he?

Fergus blushes. He buries himself in his drink.

DIL: Just cut his hair, you know.

COL: Yeah?

DIL: What you think?

COL: Nice.

Fergus throws his eyes toward her again. She has her face turned away, but sees him in the mirror.

DIL: There, he did it again.

COL: Saw that one.

DIL: What would you call it?

COL: Now, that *was* a look.

She eyes Fergus in the mirror.

DIL: Ask him to ask me what I'm drinking.

The barman, with infinite weariness, approaches Fergus.

COL: She wants to know do you want to know what she's drinking.

Fergus is about to talk when she pipes up.

DIL: A margarita.

The barman mixes it. She stares at the mirror, staring at Fergus, who is trying to avoid her eyes. The barman hands her the drink.

DIL: Now he can look. . . . Ask him does he like his hair, Col.

COL: She wants to know, sir, do you like your hair.

FERGUS: Tell her I'm very happy with it.

DIL: He's Scottish, Col.

COL: Scottish?

FERGUS: Yeah.

DIL: What'd he say, Col?

COL: He agreed that he was.

DIL: What do you think his name is?

COL: I've no thoughts on the subject.

FERGUS: Jimmy.

DIL: Jimmy?

COL: That's what he said. Jimmy.

DIL: Hi, Jimmy.

FERGUS: Hiya, Dil.

A burly man sits down beside her. He puts his hand on her knee.

MAN: Sing the song, Dil—

She slaps the hand away.

DIL: Fuck off, Dave.

DAVE: C'mon, babe! You know what I like . . . Easy!

She turns back to Fergus and finds his seat empty.

EXTERIOR. METRO—NIGHT.

*Fergus, standing across the road from the pub. He is sweating.
Dil comes out of the pub. She looks this way and that, as if
searching for Fergus. Fergus stands back into a shadow.*

*Dave, the burly man, comes out. He grabs her by the elbow. She
shrugs him off. She walks off. Dave follows, grabs her by the
elbow again. The sense of an old argument. Dave suddenly
strikes her across the face with his open palm. She leans her head
against a wall. Dave then puts his arms around her, consoles her.*

EXTERIOR. STREET—NIGHT.

Dave walking, holding Dil by the arm. The street is dilapidated, full of squats. They stop outside a door. Dil opens the door with a key from her purse and they both walk inside.

Fergus stands there, observing.

A light comes on in an upstairs room. Dil enters; we see her shadow in silhouette behind the curtain and the shadow of Dave coming in behind her. He begins to remove her blouse. She stands absolutely still as he does so.

Fergus backs away, then walks off.

INTERIOR. HOSTEL—NIGHT.

Fergus, in bed. Fade to black as we see Jody as a bowler, running in slow motion, toward the camera. He releases the ball; we see Fergus in bed, breathing heavily.

INTERIOR. SITE—NEXT DAY.

Fergus takes a break and watches the batsman hit a ball. He imitates the batsman's motion with his sledgehammer. Then a voice interrupts him.

DEVEROUX: So Pat's a cricket fan, eh?

Fergus turns. We see Tristram Deveroux, a young Sloane type in a three-piece suit, whose house it is. Beside him is Franknum, the cockney foreman.

FERGUS: It's not Pat. It's Jim.

DEVEROUX: Jim, Pat, Mick, what the fuck. Long as you remember you're not at Lords.

Fergus resumes work.

INTERIOR. METRO—NIGHT.

It is now crowded with people, black, white, punky and street-chic, a lot of leather. All the women are heavily made-up. Some-

one is singing from the tiny stage and rows of cheap colored bulbs are flashing around it.

From the way Fergus walks through, it is obvious he has never been here at night. He seems most out of place in his cheap suit, making his way through the crowd to the bar.

AT THE BAR.

Fergus looks through the odd crowd, but can't find Dil. Col, the barman, sees him and smiles.

COL: So can we consider you a regular, sir?

FERGUS: Is that good or bad?

COL: Well, you get to say, The usual, Col. Things like that.

Col pushes a colored cocktail with one of those Japanese umbrellas toward him.

COL: So let's call this the usual.

FERGUS: Thanks.

Fergus reaches for his wallet to pay, but Col interrupts.

COL: No, no. It's on me.

Fergus tries to pretend he's familiar with the drink, and by implication, whatever are the norms of the place. He lifts the glass to his mouth, but the umbrella keeps getting in the way.

COL: Take it out, if you want.

Fergus takes out the umbrella. He holds it in one hand and drinks with the other.

COL: You came to see her, didn't you?

Fergus shrugs. He takes out a cigarette. A guy in leather to his left smiles at him.

COL: Something I should tell you. She's——

FERGUS: She's what?

The barman looks up toward the stage.

COL: She's on.

THE JUKEBOX.

A hand presses a button. The needle selects a disk. A song by Dave Berry, "The Crying Game."

AT THE BAR.

Fergus looks up. Close-up of Dil's hand, as music begins, making movements to the music. We see Dil, standing on a stage, swaying slightly. She seems a little drunk. She mimes to the song. She mouths the words so perfectly and the voice on the song is so feminine that there is no way of knowing who is doing the singing. She does all sorts of strange movements, as if she is drawing moonbeams with her hands.

The crowd seems to know this act. They cheer, whether out of approval or derision we can't be sure.

Fergus watching.

Dil singing, noticing him. She comes to the end of the song. The crowd cheers.

Fergus, watching her make her way through the crowded bar, toward him.

DIL: He's still looking, Col.

COL: Persistent.

DIL: Good thing in a man.

COL: An excellent quality.

DIL: Maybe he wants something.

COL: I would expect he does.

DIL: Ask him.

COL: Ask him yourself.

She looks at Fergus directly, sits down next to him.

DIL: So tell me.

Fergus says nothing. He shrugs.

DIL: Everybody wants something.

FERGUS: Not me.

DIL: Not you. How quaint. How old-fashioned and quaint. Isn't it, Col?

Col shrugs.

DIL: You old-fashioned?

FERGUS: Must be.

The burly man comes up to her.

MAN: Got the money, Dil?

DIL: Fuck off, Dave.

DAVE: You fucking promised.

DIL: Did I?

DAVE: You fucking did.

He suddenly jerks her roughly off the stool, spilling her drink.

DAVE: Didn't you? Well, come on!

He drags her through the crowd. In the mirror, Fergus watches them go. The barman eyes him.

COL: It takes all types.

FERGUS: So who's he?

The Crying Game   217

COL: He's what she should run a mile from.

FERGUS: Then why doesn't she?

COL: Who knows the secrets of the human heart.

Fergus suddenly stands and makes his way to the door.

EXTERIOR. PUB—NIGHT.

Fergus comes out. A black bouncer is there, but there is no sign of Dil. He walks a few yards and hears voices down an alley. He looks up it.

POV—ALLEY.

We see Dil pushing Dave away. He grabs her, turns her roughly.

DAVE: Don't be like that—

DIL: You heard me—

She beats his arms away. Money falls on the ground. She staggers away from him. He picks up the money, then runs after her.

DAVE: Got very fucking grand, haven't we—

He tries to pull her back.

DAVE: Talk to me, you stupid bitch—

They both bump into Fergus, who just stands there and doesn't move an inch. She smiles.

DIL: Hi.

FERGUS: Hi. You forgot your bag.

He holds it up to show her.

DIL: Thank you.

DAVE: Who the fuck is he?

DIL: Jimmy.

DAVE: It's him, isn't it?

DIL: Maybe.

Dave eyes Fergus. Fergus grabs his wrists and upends him on the ground.

DIL: See, they get the wrong idea.

DAVE *(from the ground)*: Cunt.

Fergus puts his foot on Dave's neck.

FERGUS: What was that?

DIL: They all get the wrong idea.

DAVE: Cunt. Scrag-eyed dyke cunt.

DIL: Charming.

Dave grabs for her ankle. She kicks his hand away. Fergus presses down his foot. He looks to Dil.

FERGUS: What'll I do?

DIL: Break his neck.

Fergus presses his foot.

DIL: No, don't.

She bends low to Dave.

DIL: He's going to take his foot off slowly, David. Then you're to go home, like a good boy. You hear me?

DAVE: Cunt.

But his voice is softer. Fergus removes his foot. Dil grabs his arm.

DIL: Come on, honey.

She draws him away.

EXTERIOR. METRO—NIGHT.

They walk out of the alley.

FERGUS: You all right?

DIL: Yes, thank you.

FERGUS: What was that all about?

DIL: He wants me to perform for him.

FERGUS: Perform?

DIL: You know.

FERGUS: You on the game?

DIL: God no. I'm a hairdresser.

Fergus looks back. Dave is rising.

FERGUS: He's getting up.

DIL: You can't leave me then, can you?

EXTERIOR. STAIRCASE OUTSIDE DIL'S FLAT

Fergus and Dil climb slowly upstairs.

DIL: You want me to ask you in, right?

FERGUS: No, I didn't—

DIL: But I'm not cheap, you know that? Loud, but never cheap.

There is a movement lower down the staircase. We see Dave, holding his neck.

DAVE: Fucking dumb dyke carrot cunt.

Dil leans close to Fergus.

DIL: If you kissed me, it would really get his goat.

She tilts up her face. Fergus kisses her, tenderly.

DIL: Now, if you asked me to meet you tomorrow, it would really drive him insane.

FERGUS: Where?

DIL: Half-five. At Millie's.

She goes in and closes the door. Fergus stands and looks down at Dave, who turns to leave.

EXTERIOR. HAIR SALON—DAY.

Dil walks out of the salon, smiling, and walks toward Fergus.

DIL: Give me that look again.

FERGUS: What look?

DIL: The one you gave me in the Metro.

Fergus takes a bunch of flowers from behind his back. She holds them, with theatrical feeling.

DIL: Darling, you shouldn't have.

She laughs and leans toward him and kisses him in a classically old-fashioned way. The girls inside the salon pull back a curtain, and they all clap.

FERGUS: What's that about?

DIL: They're jealous.

FERGUS: Why?

DIL: I wonder.

She takes his arm and walks off with him.

INTERIOR. INDIAN RESTAURANT—NIGHT.

Fergus and Dil looking at their menus. A waiter places drinks on their table, then leaves.

DIL: Now's the time you're meant to do something, isn't it?

FERGUS: Like what?

DIL: Make a pass or something. Isn't that the way it goes?

FERGUS: Must be.

EXTERIOR. STREET—NIGHT.

They are walking in an alleyway toward her house.

DIL: You got a special friend, Jimmy?

FERGUS: How special?

DIL: You want one?

And suddenly a car drives very fast toward them, headlights on. Fergus pulls her into a doorway to avoid it.

FERGUS: Jesus Christ!

DIL: Jesus.

The car continues down the road, stops, and then screeches off.

FERGUS: That Dave?

DIL: The things a girl has to put up with.

She looks down toward where the car has pulled away.

DIL: I'm frightened, Jimmy. That's not like him.

EXTERIOR. DIL'S FLAT.

A car pulls up behind Dil and Fergus.

DIL: Piss off, Dave!

FERGUS: Tough guy, huh? Are you going to be all right on your own?

DIL: I'm not on my own, am I?

She touches his cheek.

DIL: Come on up, would you?

INTERIOR. DIL'S FLAT—NIGHT.

Dil comes in in the darkness. Fergus stands like a shadow in the doorway. The light comes on; she takes off her raincoat.

DIL: Won't hurt you to come in.

Fergus enters slowly. He looks around the room; there is an exaggerated femininity about everything in it.

DIL: Would you like a drink?

FERGUS: Yes, please.

DIL: What'll it be?

FERGUS: Whiskey.

She goes into a small kitchen. Fergus looks at the mantelpiece and sees a picture of Jody. The camera tracks into the soldier's smiling face. Then into Fergus's face. His reverie is broken by the sound of a voice outside—Dave's.

She comes through with two drinks.

FERGUS: Someone out there.

DIL: Jesus fucking Christ.

She opens the window door, and we see Dave on the street, in a neck brace.

DIL: Hey, Stirling fucking Moss—

DAVE: It's Dave.

She goes back into the room and begins taking things up.

DAVE: Talk to me, Dil—

DIL: Sure, Dave—

DAVE: Please, Dil—

She flings things down: men's clothes, leather trousers, a suitcase, a teddy bear.

DIL: Take your clothes.

DAVE: Don't throw my clothes out the window!

DIL: Fuck off back to Essex!

DAVE: Fucking mad!

Fergus looks to the man down in the street, a parody of rejection with his things in his arms.

DAVE: Don't chuck my clothes out!

DIL: Take your fucking goldfish, too!

Dil grabs a large goldfish bowl and flings it down. The bowl breaks to bits on the pavement. Goldfish thrash around in the street.

DAVE: You fucking bitch!

He tries to pick up the flapping fish in his hands.

DAVE: Murderer!

Upstairs, Dil closes the window shut.

DIL: Sorry. How'd he drive with his neck in a brace?

FERGUS: Must be in love to manage that.

DIL: Doesn't know the meaning of the word.

Fergus stands as Dil hands him a glass.

FERGUS: He lived here with you?

DIL: Tried to. Sit down, will you?

Fergus walks past the photograph and sits down. He looks from her to the picture.

FERGUS: What about him?

He nods toward the picture. She looks down into her drink.

DIL: He was different.

FERGUS: How different?

DIL: As different as it's possible to be.

FERGUS: Tell me about him.

DIL: No.

FERGUS: Shouldn't I go?

DIL: Yes.

And they fall into one another's arms. She stretches up with her whole body over him. They grow suddenly and violently passionate.

They fall into the cushions of the couch onto the floor. The photograph above them seems to smile. He draws up her dress with his hands. She suddenly pulls away.

DIL: No—

FERGUS: Did you do that to him?

She comes up toward him once more. She puts her mouth close to his ear.

DIL: You want to know how I kissed him?

FERGUS: Yes . . .

DIL: Are you jealous of him?

FERGUS: Maybe.

DIL: That's good . . .

She opens the buttons on his shirt and her mouth travels down his chest. Fergus tries to draw her up toward him, but her hand reaches up to his mouth and presses his head back while her other hand undoes his pants. She kisses his stomach; her mouth moves down his body. Fergus stares at the picture of Jody. Jody's eyes seem to burn through him. Dil raises her head and kisses his mouth. There are tears in his eyes.

FERGUS: What would he think?

DIL: Can't think. He's dead. In Ireland. He was a soldier. Went there like a fool.

She sits in front of the mirror.

FERGUS: Do you miss him?

DIL: What do you think?

FERGUS: I think you do.

DIL (*dreamily*): You say that like a gentleman.

FERGUS: Do I?

DIL: Like you're concerned.

Fergus gets up and stands behind her, gently pushes the hair from her face.

DIL: But you can't stay, you know that?

FERGUS: Didn't think I could.

DIL: A real gentleman . . .

She embraces him.

FERGUS: Shouldn't you be in mourning?

DIL: I am.

She sits back down in front of the mirror. Fergus leaves. She reapplies her lipstick.

INTERIOR. METRO—NIGHT.

Singer in a blue dress. Dil and Fergus by the bar. Both drinking drinks with umbrellas. Dave comes up behind them with his neck brace.

DAVE: Look, I'm sorry.

DIL: Fuck off, Dave.

DAVE: No, I won't fucking fuck off. Said I'm sorry, didn't I?

DIL: Yeah. I heard. You hear, Jimmy?

Fergus nods. He stands. Dave steps two feet back.

FERGUS: I was only going to ask her for a dance.

Fergus takes Dil's arm.

FERGUS: Shall we?

The woman is singing.

As they circle, people begin to look at them admiringly. Dil holds her cheek close to his.

FERGUS: Did he come here too?

DIL: Is this an obsession of yours?

FERGUS: Maybe.

DIL: He did sometimes.

FERGUS: Did he dance with you?

Dil doesn't answer. Looks at him out of the corner of her eye.

DIL: So what do you want with me, Jimmy?

FERGUS: Want to look after you.

DIL: What does that mean?

FERGUS: Something I heard someone say once.

She draws back and looks at him.

DIL: You mean that?

FERGUS: Yeah.

She dances closer.

DIL: Why?

FERGUS: If I told you, you wouldn't believe me.

In the bar, people singing along with the music. Col sings. Dave sitting at the bar, sulking.

DIL: You're not having me on, are you? 'Cause Dil can't stand that.

FERGUS: No.

She puts her cheek against his. Dave, at the bar, slams his drink down.

DIL: And she does get very upset . . .

Dave stands up to leave. On the stage the act finishes. Dil draws Fergus back to the bar.

AT THE BAR.

Col, the barman, pours her drink.

DIL: One for him, too.

Col pours and smiles.

DIL: Drink.

FERGUS: What is this?

DIL: I'm superstitious. Drink.

He drinks. He grimaces. She throws it back in one.

DIL: Can't leave me now.

FERGUS: Aha.

DIL: The thing is, can you go the distance?

FERGUS: Depends what it is.

DIL: No, depends on nothing.

She takes the bottle herself and fills their glasses. She slams it back. He sips.

DIL: In one.

She tilts his glass back. He swallows it in one.

INTERIOR. DIL'S FLAT—NIGHT.

She enters; Fergus walks in slowly. He looks from the cricket whites that are hanging up behind a curtain to the photographs.

DIL: What you thinking of, hon?

FERGUS: I'm thinking of your man.

DIL: Why?

FERGUS: I'm wondering why you keep his things.

DIL: Told you, I'm superstitious.

She turns toward him and undoes her hair. It falls around her shoulders.

FERGUS: Did he ever tell you you were beautiful?

DIL: All the time.

Fergus runs his hand down her throat.

DIL: Even now.

FERGUS: No . . .

DIL: He looks after me. He's a gentleman too.

She draws him behind a curtain toward the bed, pulls him down. They kiss passionately.

DIL: Give me one minute.

She walks into the bathroom. Fergus lies there, looking at the picture, listening to the sound of running water. She comes out then, dressed in a silk kimono. She looks extraordinarily beautiful. He reaches out his hand and grasps hers. He draws her toward him. He begins to kiss her face and neck.

FERGUS: Would he have minded?

She murmurs no. His hands slip the wrap down from her shoulders.

CLOSE ON HIS HANDS, *traveling down her neck, in the darkness. Then the hands stop. The kimono falls to the floor gently, with a whisper. The camera travels with it, and we see, in a close-up, that she is a man.*

Fergus sits there, frozen, staring at her.

DIL: You did know, didn't you?

Fergus says nothing.

DIL: Oh my God.

She gives a strange little laugh, then reaches out to touch him. Fergus smacks the hand away.

FERGUS: Jesus. I feel sick—

He gets up and runs to the bathroom. She grabs his feet.

DIL: Don't go, Jimmy—

He kicks her away. He runs into the bathroom and vomits into the tub.

She crouches on the floor.

DIL: I'm sorry. I thought you knew.

He retches again.

DIL: What were you doing in the bar if you didn't know? . . . I'm
bleeding . . .

She lights a cigarette.

Fergus runs the taps. He washes his face, rinses his mouth.

DIL: It's all right, Jimmy. I can take it. Just not on the face.

*Fergus slams the door shut. She is sitting on the couch, the
kimono round her once more, looking very much like a woman.
A trace of blood on her mouth.*

DIL: Y'see, I'm not a young thing any longer. . . . Funny the way
things go. Don't you find that, Jimmy? Never the way you
expected.

Fergus comes out of the bathroom.

FERGUS: I'm sorry.

She looks up. Some hope in her face.

DIL: You mean that?

And he makes to go. She grabs him to stop him.

DIL: Don't go like that. Say something . . .

He pulls away from her. She falls to the floor.

DIL: Jesus.

He drags himself away and runs down the stairs.

INTERIOR. FERGUS'S FLAT

*Fergus in bed. Flash to shot of blackness, Jody grinning in
cricket whites, throwing the ball up and down in his hand.*

INTERIOR. METRO—NIGHT.

*The place is hopping. Fergus enters. He now sees it as he should
have seen it the first night—as a transvestite bar. He makes his*

way through the crowds. All the women too-heavily made-up. Some beautifully sleek young things he looks at he realizes are young men. He makes his way to the bar where Dil is sitting, nursing a drink with an umbrella in it. Her face is bruised. She is wearing dark glasses.

As he walks toward her she sees him in the mirror. She talks to Col, the barman.

DIL: He's back, Col.

COL: Hi.

DIL: Don't want any of those looks, Col. They don't mean much.

COL: Stop it, Dil—

DIL: No. Tell him to go fuck himself.

Fergus sits. Col turns to him.

COL: She wants me to tell you go fuck yourself.

FERGUS: I'm sorry.

There is a tear running down her cheek, under the dark glasses.

DIL: Tell him to stop messing Dil around—

FERGUS: Dil—

DIL: Tell him it hurt—

FERGUS: I have to talk to her, Col—

COL: Says he's got to talk to you—

Fergus touches her arm.

FERGUS: Come on, Dil—

DIL: Where?

She whips her arm away.

DIL: Tell him again, Col. Go fuck himself—

She walks into the crowd, toward the door.

Fergus leaves.

EXTERIOR. STREET—NIGHT.

Fergus, walking outside Dil's place. The blinds in her room are down and the light is on inside. We see her outline, pacing up and down behind the blinds, smoking a cigarette. We hear the song "The Crying Game."

Fergus stands beneath her doorway, scribbles a note, and sticks it in the letter box.

EXTERIOR. CRICKET PITCH—DAY.

A man removes a large number six from a huge scoreboard with a pole and replaces it with a number nine.

Below the scoreboard we can see Dil walking across a lawn toward the building where Fergus is working.

INTERIOR. SITE—DAY.

Fergus, fitting a new window into the finished wall. On the pitch we see the cricketers, distorted through the moving glass of the window. Across the pitch Dil walks, with a lunch basket in her hand, dressed in a very short skirt with high heels. As she approaches the site a chorus of whistles breaks out.

Fergus, hearing the whistling, stares out. He sees Dil moving toward the site. He drops the window and the glass shatters. As the whistles continue, we see Dil in the site's lift, which rises up. We see Deveroux and Franknum climbing up a ladder toward Fergus.

DEVEROUX: How much did that frame cost, Mr. Franknum?

FRANKNUM: Two hundred quid, Mr. Deveroux.

DEVEROUX: Your Pat just cost me two hundred quid.

FERGUS: Sorry.

DEVEROUX: Sorry won't bring the bloody thing back, will it, Mr. Franknum?

FRANKNUM: Not in my experience.

DEVEROUX: Off his wages.

FERGUS: Do you mean that?

DEVEROUX: He wants to know do I mean that.

FRANKNUM: I'm sure you do, Mr. Deveroux.

DEVEROUX: Bloody right I do . . .

Through this conversation Fergus can hear the chorus of wolf whistles increasing. He looks out the gap where the window should be and sees Dil in the lift. The laborers whistle at her, looking up her skirt, etc.

She passes by a gap in the wall and blows a kiss at him.

DEVEROUX: Is that his tart? Does Pat have a tart?

FERGUS: She's not a tart.

DEVEROUX: No, of course not, she's a lady.

FERGUS: She's not that either.

Fergus walks out of the room.

Fergus walks round the scaffolding. Dil sees him and waves, sits on some bricks and opens the hamper.

DIL: Darling—

She is acting bright and businesslike, like any wife. She is wearing dark glasses to cover the bruise on her face. She pecks him on the cheek.

DIL: Never let the sun go down on an argument, Jody used to say.

FERGUS: What you doing here?

DIL: Got your note. So let's kiss and make up, hon.

FERGUS: Don't call me that.

DIL: Sorry, darling.

FERGUS: Give it over, Dil—

DIL: Apologies, my sweet.

Fergus smiles in spite of himself.

DIL: That's more like it, dear. Have a cuppa.

She takes out a thermos and pours him some tea.

FERGUS: You're something else, Dil, you know that?

DIL: Never said a truer word.

She hands him a neatly cut sandwich.

DIL: See, I was always best looking after someone. Must be something in the genes.

FERGUS: Must be.

DIL: And the fact that you didn't know is basically the fault of yours truly. And even when you were throwing up, I could tell you cared.

FERGUS: You could?

DIL: Do you care, Jimmy?

FERGUS: Sure I do.

DIL: You mean that?

FERGUS: Yeah. I care, Dil.

She lowers her head.

FERGUS: You crying, Dil?

He removes her glasses and looks at her moist eyes.

DIL: I'm tired and emotional.

Then he hears a voice behind him.

DEVEROUX: Do it on your own time, Paddy.

FERGUS: What?

DEVEROUX: Whatever it is she does for you.

Fergus looks from Dil to Deveroux.

FERGUS: If I was her I'd consider that an insult.

DEVEROUX: Consider it how you like. Just get that bloody tart out of here.

Fergus stands up suddenly. He speaks quietly.

FERGUS: Did you ever pick your teeth up with broken fingers?

Deveroux stares, suddenly chilled.

DEVEROUX: What's that supposed to mean?

FERGUS: It's a simple question.

Deveroux says nothing. Fergus looks down to Dil.

FERGUS: Come on, dear.

He holds out his arm. Dil gathers up her things and takes it. Her face is wreathed in a smile.

DIL: He didn't answer, honey—

Fergus walks her down the scaffolding ramp.

FRANKNUM: Sorry about that, Mr. Deveroux.

Dil and Fergus descend from the site in the lift.

DIL: My, oh my, Jimmy, how gallant.

FERGUS: Shut up.

DIL: Made me feel all funny inside.

FERGUS: I said stop it.

DIL: Ask me to meet you again, Jimmy.

FERGUS: You think that's wise?

DIL: Nothing's wise.

The lift stops with a thud.

FERGUS: I didn't mean to hit you.

DIL: I know that.

FERGUS: Kind of liked you as a girl.

DIL: That's a start.

FERGUS: So I'm sorry.

DIL: Make it up to me, then.

FERGUS: How?

DIL: Ask to meet me again.

FERGUS: Will you meet me again?

DIL: When?

FERGUS: Whenever. Tonight.

She leans forward and kisses him. Fergus hears a wail of catcalls behind him. He watches Dil go as the lift takes him back up to the site.

EXTERIOR. HAIR SALON—EVENING.

Fergus, outside the hair salon. Dil, inside, is throwing off her smock and walking toward him. All the girls are smiling. Fergus looks from Dil to the girls as they approach.

FERGUS: Do they know?

DIL: Know what, honey?

FERGUS: Know what I didn't know. And don't call me that.

DIL: Can't help it, Jimmy. A girl has her feelings.

FERGUS: Thing is, Dil, you're not a girl.

DIL: Details, baby, details.

FERGUS: So they do know.

DIL: All right, they do.

She takes his arm as they walk off.

FERGUS: Don't.

DIL: Sorry.

FERGUS: I should have known, shouldn't I?

DIL: Probably.

FERGUS: Kind of wish I didn't.

DIL: You can always pretend.

FERGUS: That's true. . . . Your soldier knew, didn't he?

DIL: Absolutely.

FERGUS: Won't be quite the same though, will it?

DIL: Are you pretending yet?

FERGUS: I'm working on it.

Fergus hears a car following them, and turns around to look.

FERGUS: There's Dave. He knew too.

DIL: Stop it, Jimmy.

FERGUS: Am I becoming repetitious?

DIL: A little.

FERGUS: Sorry.

They reach her door. The car stops.

FERGUS: Don't ask me in.

DIL: Please, Jimmy.

FERGUS: No. Can't pretend that much.

DIL: I miss you, Jimmy.

FERGUS: Should have stayed a girl.

DIL: Don't be cruel.

FERGUS: Okay. Be a good girl and go inside.

DIL: Only if you kiss me.

Fergus kisses her. He looks at her open lips as if in disbelief at himself.

FERGUS: Happy now?

DIL: Delirious.

She goes inside.

INTERIOR. HOSTEL—NIGHT.

Fergus walks into the room and turns on a small desk-light. Then he hears a voice.

JUDE: Hello, stranger.

He sees Jude sitting in the corner. Her hair is now dark brown.

JUDE: You vanished.

He stares at her, says nothing.

JUDE: What was it, Fergus? Did you blow the gaff on us or did you just fuck up?

FERGUS: Leave me alone, Jude.

JUDE: No. That's the last thing I'll do. You never asked what happened.

FERGUS: I heard.

JUDE: Eddie and Tinker died.

FERGUS: I know.

JUDE: Maguire and me got out by the skin of our teeth. No thanks to you. . . . What you think of the hair?

FERGUS: Suits you.

She walks round the room.

JUDE: Aye, I was sick of being blond. Needed a tougher look, if you know what I mean.

She lies down on the bed beside him, takes off a black leather glove, and puts her hand on his crotch.

JUDE: Fuck me, Fergus.

He takes her hand away.

JUDE: Am I to take it that's a no?

He says nothing.

JUDE: We had a court-martial in your absence. They wanted to put a bullet in your head. I pleaded for clemency. Said we should find out what happened first. So what did happen?

FERGUS: He ran. I couldn't shoot him in the back. I tried to catch him. He made it to the road and got hit by a Saracen.

JUDE: So you did fuck up.

FERGUS: Yes.

JUDE: But you know what the thing is, Fergus?

FERGUS: No, what is the thing?

JUDE: You vanished quite effectively. Became Mister Nobody. And you've no idea how useful that could be.

FERGUS: What do you mean?

JUDE: We've got some plans here. And we'll need a Mister Nobody to execute them.

FERGUS: No way, Jude. I'm out.

JUDE: You're never out, Fergus.

She looks at him hard. He looks away.

JUDE: Maybe you don't care whether you die or not. But consider the girl, Fergus. The wee black chick.

He leaps up from the bed.

FERGUS: Leave her out of this.

JUDE: Jesus, Fergus, you're a walking cliché. You know we won't leave her out of this. But I'm glad to see you care.

She brings her lips close to his so they touch.

JUDE: And I must admit I'm curious.

He grabs her hair and pulls her head back.

FERGUS: What the fuck do you know, Jude?

She pulls a gun and sticks it between his teeth.

JUDE: You fucking tell me, boy—

Fergus stares at her. Then says quietly:

FERGUS: She's nobody. She likes me.

JUDE: So I suppose a fuck is out of the question. Keep your head down, Fergus. No sudden moves. And not a whisper to her. You'll be hearing from us.

She kisses him briefly, with the gun at his temple.

JUDE: Keep the faith.

She goes. Fergus stands in the darkness.

EXTERIOR. HAIR SALON—EVENING.

Fergus, walking toward the hair salon, flowers in his hand.

He stands outside watching, the flowers behind his back. Then the chair turns and we see it is Jude.

Fergus freezes. He sees Jude looking at him, smiling brightly, then talking back to Dil.

INTERIOR. HAIR SALON—EVENING.

JUDE: He your boyfriend?

Jude, turning in the chair.

JUDE: Lucky you.

INTERIOR. INDIAN RESTAURANT—NIGHT.

DIL: Carnations.

FERGUS: What?

DIL: He'd bring me carnations.

FERGUS: So I got it wrong, then.

DIL: Not at all, honey.

FERGUS: Don't.

DIL: Okay.

She smiles brightly at something behind Fergus. He turns and sees Jude is there. Fergus stands, suddenly.

He throws some money on the table, grabs her arm, and frog-marches her out.

FERGUS: Come on.

DIL: Why, honey—

FERGUS: Come on.

DIL: You gonna tell me why?

FERGUS: No.

As they pass Jude, she smiles.

EXTERIOR. INDIAN RESTAURANT—NIGHT.

Outside the restaurant. Fergus marches Dil away.

DIL: What's wrong, Jimmy? Tell me what's wrong—

FERGUS: Not here.

They pass out of shot. In the background we see Jude rising.

INTERIOR. METRO—NIGHT.

Dil and Fergus making their way to their seats at the bar.

DIL: You gonna tell me what it is?

A figure sitting down at the bar. It is Jude.

JUDE: What was it?

DIL: You know her, Jimmy?

JUDE: Jimmy, is it? Do you know me, Jimmy?

FERGUS: Dil, this is Jude.

DIL: You following me?

JUDE: Yeah. Just checking. He being nice to you, Dil?

DIL: Ever so nice. Aren't you, Jimmy?

JUDE: That's good. I'm glad. Young love, as they say.

DIL: Absolutely. The younger the better. Doesn't come your way much, I suppose.

JUDE: Don't go looking for it, Dil.

DIL: Well, maybe you'll get lucky. Someday.

JUDE: A bit heavy on the powder, isn't she, Jimmy?

DIL: A girl has to have a bit of glamour.

JUDE: Absolutely. Long as she can keep it. Isn't that right, James . . .

She leaves. Dil watches her go.

DIL: It's her, isn't it?

FERGUS: What's her?

DIL: She's the thing you had to tell me.

FERGUS: Kind of.

DIL: I'm sorry, you know that? I'm really sorry.

She looks at Col.

DIL: You see that, Col?

COL: Saw it, Dil.

DIL: Fuck it, is what I say.

COL: Yeah. Fuck it, Dil.

DIL: Fucking men, Col.

COL: Fuck 'em.

There are tears in her eyes. She stands.

DIL: And fuck you, Jimmy—

She staggers out of the pub. Fergus sits there. There is an expression in Col's eyes that makes Fergus feel very, very small.

COL: You could always make it up to her.

FERGUS: How?

COL: When a girl runs out like that, she generally wants to be followed.

FERGUS: She's not a girl, Col.

COL: Whatever you say.

But Fergus rises and walks out.

EXTERIOR. METRO—NIGHT.

A figure standing down the alleyway, smoking. Fergus looks toward it, but Jude is standing there, waiting.

JUDE: She went that way—

Jude grabs his arm.

JUDE: But you come with me.

She draws him down an alley where the same car is waiting. They get inside.

ANOTHER CAR—BY THE PUB.

Dil, sitting inside a taxi watching Fergus and Jude getting in the car.

INTERIOR. CAR—NIGHT.

In the moving car. Jude is driving, Maguire next to her. Fergus sits in the back.

FERGUS: So it was you all the time.

MAGUIRE: Who'd you think it was?

FERGUS: I thought it was Dave.

MAGUIRE: And who's Dave when he's at home?

FERGUS: He's at home.

MAGUIRE: Should blow you away, you know that?

FERGUS: I know that.

Maguire stubs his cigarette out on Fergus's hand, then whacks him on the teeth with his closed fist.

MAGUIRE: I'm getting emotional. And I don't want to get fucking emotional—you understand, Hennessy?

FERGUS: I understand.

MAGUIRE: Fuck you, too—

Jude drives. Fergus looks through the back window at the street outside.

JUDE: Leave him alone, Peter. He's in love.

MAGUIRE: That true, Fergus? You in love?

FERGUS: Absolutely.

MAGUIRE: And what's she like between the sheets?

FERGUS: Definitely unusual.

MAGUIRE: And who is she?

FERGUS: Just a girl.

MAGUIRE: And you know what'll happen if you fuck up again, don't you?

FERGUS: Aye, I do, Peter.

MAGUIRE: Good.

EXTERIOR. REGENCY SQUARE—NIGHT.

The car draws to a halt in a sedate square. Several doors down is the entrance to what looks like a sedate conservative club.

In the car, Maguire turns off the engine. He nods toward the building.

MAGUIRE: So what do you think that is, Hennessy?

FERGUS: A hotel?

MAGUIRE: It's a knocking-shop. *Très* discreet, huh? He visits his ladies on Tuesday and Thursday nights and Saturday mornings. His security's in the car beyond.

He nods toward a car, a Daimler, parked some distance away. Fergus looks from the window to the car.

FERGUS: Who is he?

MAGUIRE: Doesn't matter who he is. He is what we would call a legitimate target.

FERGUS: Thank God for that.

MAGUIRE: You being cynical, Hennessy?

FERGUS: Hope not.

MAGUIRE: Good. So what do you think?

FERGUS: Whoever hits him'll be hit, if those men are any good. And I presume you can't get in.

MAGUIRE: Right.

FERGUS: So it's on the street.

MAGUIRE: Right.

FERGUS: Kind of suicide, isn't it?

Jude turns around to look at him.

FERGUS: But, then, I don't have a choice.

JUDE: Och, you do, Fergie.

FERGUS: Of course. I forgot.

JUDE: Come on, Fergie. A rehearsal.

Jude and Fergus get out of the car. They walk down the street, down from the brothel-cum-club, where there is a café-bar with some tables outside.

EXTERIOR. REGENCY SQUARE—NIGHT.

Fergus and Jude, crossing the street.

JUDE: You keep your mind on the job, boy—

FERGUS: And then you'll leave her out of it?

JUDE: Aye. Then we'll leave her be.

They take their seats by the tables. We can see the brothel down the way.

JUDE: He's arthritic. Takes him two minutes to get to the door.

She checks her watch. Fergus is sweating.

FERGUS: And what if I say no?

JUDE: You know what. Go.

Down by the brothel, the door swings open.

Fergus walks like any pedestrian down toward the brothel. There is an old, portly gent in a City suit emerging from it. The car by the pavement kicks into action and the door opens.

Fergus quickens his pace.

Jude, by the café, watches.

Fergus, walking.

The gent makes his way, with gout-ridden slowness, across the pavement, through the passersby, toward the car.

A burly security man emerging from the car, walking toward the old gent.

Fergus reaches the car just before he does, and passes between him and the open door. The old gent's stomach brushes Fergus's elbow.

GENT: Pardon me, young man—

Fergus walks on.

Jude, from the café, watches—Fergus walking on, the old man being eased with painstaking care inside the Daimler. Then the door closing and the Daimler pulling off.

When the Daimler has passed Fergus, he turns around and walks back.

Jude smiles and leaps up as he approaches.

JUDE: You were made for this.

FERGUS: Was I?

JUDE: Perfect.

FERGUS: And what happens then?

JUDE: We'll be on the other side. We'll move when you do.

FERGUS: And what if you don't?

JUDE: Fergus, I think you don't trust me.

FERGUS: You may be right.

JUDE: Stay late at your work tomorrow night and I'll bring you the gear.

Jude begins to walk away.

FERGUS: Jude?

JUDE: Yes?

FERGUS: Who's the old geezer?

JUDE: Some judge . . .

She walks off, crosses the road to Maguire, in the car. Fergus turns around to see Dil, in front of the café. She goes inside; he follows.

FERGUS: Why'd you follow me, Dil?

DIL: Was jealous, Jimmy.

She downs a drink and motions for another. She seems high.

FERGUS: Shouldn't be, Dil.

DIL: Why shouldn't I be jealous?

There are tears streaming down her face. He takes his hand and begins to wipe her face.

DIL: Don't. My makeup.

She sits down; he joins her.

DIL: She own you, Jimmy?

FERGUS: Yes.

DIL: She from Scotland too?

FERGUS: You could say that.

DIL: And you're not going to tell me more?

FERGUS: I can't.

He wipes the tears from her face with a tissue then dabs the tissue in her drink and wipes some more.

DIL: What you doing, Jimmy?

FERGUS: I'm not sure.

DIL: Do you like me even a little bit?

FERGUS: More than that.

Dil's face, staring at him.

FERGUS: Come on, let's go for a walk.

She allows herself to be led out.

EXTERIOR. HAIR SALON—NIGHT.

Dil and Fergus walking. Fergus stops her by the window.

FERGUS: You do something for me, Dil?

DIL: Anything.

FERGUS: You'd do anything for me?

DIL: Afraid so.

FERGUS: You got the keys to the shop?

They walk inside.

INTERIOR. HAIR SALON—NIGHT.

Dil and Fergus standing in the darkness.

DIL: You want another haircut, baby?

FERGUS: No. Sit down.

He sits her down in one of the chairs.

FERGUS: You'd do anything for me?

Dil nods.

DIL: Anything.

Fergus takes up a scissors to snip at her hair. Her head leaps back.

DIL: No way—

FERGUS: You said anything, Dil—

DIL: A girl has to draw the line somewhere—

FERGUS: Want to change you to a man, Dil . . .

She stares at him.

DIL: Why?

FERGUS: It's a secret.

DIL: You'd like me better that way, Jimmy?

FERGUS: Yes.

DIL: And you wouldn't leave me?

FERGUS: No.

DIL: You promise?

FERGUS: I promise.

She takes a breath.

DIL: Go on, then.

Fergus begins to cut.

CLOSE-UP ON DIL'S FACE *as her hair is shorn. Tears stream down her cheeks.*

DIL: You're no good at this, Jimmy.

FERGUS: I'm sorry.

But he keeps cutting. He gives Dil a short, cropped military cut like Jody's.

DIL: You want to make me look like him . . .

FERGUS: No. Want to make you into something new. That nobody recognizes . . .

She looks in the mirror at it in the dark.

DIL: Don't recognize myself, Jimmy.

INTERIOR. DIL'S FLAT—NIGHT.

Dil enters, with her new haircut. She goes to turn on the light. He stops her hand.

FERGUS: No.

She looks at her hand on his.

FERGUS: Better in the dark.

Her fingers close around his.

DIL: So it's true, then?

FERGUS: What?

DIL: You like me better like this.

FERGUS: Yes.

She brings her lips to his neck. He lets them stay there. His hands travel up to her blouse. He begins to undo the buttons.

DIL: Oh, Jimmy—

Slowly the blouse slips down, exposing her male torso. She falls down to her knees and tugs at his belt.

FERGUS: No. No. Dil . . . get up . . .

He raises her to her feet and leads her toward the bed. She stretches languorously down on it. He unzips her skirt slowly, and draws it off. She turns on the bed sexily, her face to the mattress. She is wearing suspender-belts underneath her skirt.

DIL: Baby . . .

But Fergus stands and walks quietly over to the wardrobe where the soldier's things are. Dil, on the bed, slowly turns.

DIL: What are you doing, honey . . .

We see Fergus from her point of view, coming toward her with Jody's white cricket shirt, glowing eerily in the dark.

FERGUS: Don't call me that—

DIL: Sorry. What you doing?

Fergus draws her slowly up to a standing position.

FERGUS: Try this on, Dil.

He wraps the shirt around her.

DIL: Why?

FERGUS: For me.

DIL: For you . . .

She kisses him.

EXTERIOR. SMALL HOTEL—NIGHT.

Fergus leading Dil, dressed in Jody's cricket clothes, down the street and inside.

DIL: Why are we going here, Jimmy?

FERGUS: Look on it like a honeymoon.

INTERIOR. SMALL HOTEL ROOM—NIGHT.

From above, we see the figures of Fergus and Dil, sleeping on a double bed, both fully clothed. Fergus smokes, then puts out the cigarette.

Time lapse. The light gradually fills the room. Fergus wakes. Looks at the bedside clock, and very gingerly rises, puts on his coat, and walks out.

EXTERIOR. SITE—EVENING.

A car pulls up at the site. Jude gets out. She has a satchel in her hand.

INTERIOR. SITE—EVENING.

Fergus looking down a ladder-staircase at Jude.

JUDE: You a handyman, Fergie?

FERGUS: I take pride in my work.

JUDE: I sincerely hope so.

Fergus climbs down a ladder to Jude; she hands him something from the bag.

JUDE: Tools of the trade.

She kisses him. Fergus looks at her expressionlessly.

JUDE: And forget about the girl.

Fergus opens what Jude has given him—looking inside. There is a gun wrapped in an oilcloth.

INTERIOR. SMALL HOTEL—NIGHT.

Fergus enters. The room is empty. He calls.

FERGUS: Dil?

No reply. He runs outside.

EXTERIOR. DIL'S FLAT—NIGHT.

Fergus looks up at her building, but the lights are off in her flat. The sound of feet behind him. He turns and sees Dil walking toward him, a bottle in her hand. He runs toward her.

FERGUS: Dil! Dil! What the fuck are you doing here?

DIL: I'm going home!

FERGUS: Told you to stay in the hotel!

DIL: Thought you was fooling me. Thought you was leaving me.

They are tussling in the darkness of the park. She is very drunk.

FERGUS: I had to go to work!

DIL: Stayed all day in that room thinking every noise was you.
There's something you're not telling me, Jimmy.

He takes her arm.

FERGUS: Come on . . .

DIL: No! I'm going home . . .

Fergus and Dil, on the stairs up to Dil's flat.

DIL: So tell me.

FERGUS: I was trying to get out of something.

DIL: No! Tell me everything, Jimmy.

Fergus looks at her.

FERGUS: You got to forget you ever saw me, Dil.

DIL: You mean that?

FERGUS: Yes.

And she suddenly faints into his arms. As if on cue.

FERGUS: Stop it, would you?

There is no response. He shakes her.

FERGUS: Give it over, Dil, for fuck's sake—

*Still no response. He grows alarmed. He slaps her cheek. She
opens her eyes slowly.*

DIL: Sorry. I get nervous. I got this blood condition. Just help me
inside, Jimmy, then I'll be all right.

INTERIOR. DIL'S FLAT—NIGHT.

He walks in holding her. Leans her against the wall, then goes to the window to check the street outside.

She takes a large slug from a bottle of whiskey.

FERGUS: You heard what I said, Dil?

DIL: My pills . . .

She points weakly to a cabinet through the open door of the bathroom.

FERGUS: What pills?

DIL: Prescription. For my condition.

FERGUS: What condition?

DIL: My condition. Ennui.

He goes and gets the pills.

She takes a handful of pills. She drinks from the whiskey bottle.

FERGUS: Are you supposed to take that many?

DIL: Only in times of extreme stress.

She walks around the room, drinking, then sits down.

DIL: See, they all say good-bye sometime. 'Cept for him.

She looks at the picture of Jody. Then she looks at Fergus.

FERGUS: Are you all right, Dil?

DIL: I will be.

She stares straight ahead, the bottle clutched in her hands between her knees.

DIL: Go on, then.

Fergus walks slowly toward the door.

FERGUS: Good-bye, Dil.

DIL: Jimmy?

FERGUS: What?

DIL: Don't go like that.

She looks at him, standing up. Something incredibly attractive about her.

DIL: Can't help what I am.

He walks slowly toward her. He kisses her, on the lips.

We see the photograph with the soldier's smiling face. Fergus looks from it to her. She seems to be in a sweet narcotic haze. She reaches out her hand and strokes his.

DIL: Knew you had a heart . . .

Fergus sits down on the bed. Dil is lying back on it.

FERGUS: Dil. Can I tell you something? I knew your man.

DIL: You knew which man?

FERGUS: Your soldier.

DIL: You knew my Jody?

She still strokes his hand. Her voice is dreamily slurred, her eyes far away.

FERGUS: Lifted him from a carnival in Belfast. Held him hostage for three days.

DIL: You knew my Jody?

FERGUS: Are you listening?

Dil smiles woozily.

DIL: Yes.

FERGUS: I got the order to shoot him. Before I could do it he ran. Ran into a tank and died.

DIL: Died . . .

FERGUS: Did you hear me?

DIL: You killed my Jody?

FERGUS: In a manner of speaking.

DIL: It was you . . .

She is not rational. She is smiling, far away somewhere.

FERGUS: You should scream. You should beat my head off.

She woozily tries to hit him round the face.

DIL: You killed my Jody.

FERGUS: No.

DIL: You didn't.

FERGUS: I suppose I tried.

DIL: You tried.

FERGUS: Don't you want to kill me?

Dil raises an unsteady hand and points it at him.

DIL: Bang . . .

He strokes her cheek. She says very slowly and sleepily:

DIL: Don't leave me tonight. Might kill me, too.

FERGUS: Okay.

Her eyes close. She falls into a deep sleep. Fergus looks down at her, almost fondly.

INTERIOR. DIL'S FLAT—MORNING.

They are lying on the bed together, fully clothed. Dil wakes. She rises very quietly and goes to his coat, thrown across a chair. She searches through the pockets and takes out the gun.

INTERIOR. HOTEL ROOM—MORNING.

Jude in bed. An alarm sounds; she reaches to turn it off.

INTERIOR. DIL'S FLAT.

Dil takes several silk stockings out of a drawer and ties them very securely to each corner of the brass bed. She ties them round both of Fergus's feet, very gently, so as not to wake him.

INTERIOR. HOTEL ROOM—MORNING.

Jude, in front of a mirror, getting ready.

INTERIOR. DIL'S FLAT.

She draws one of Fergus's hands up, very gingerly, and ties that securely to the upright. She ties the other and is drawing it upward when he wakes. She jerks the silk stocking so it is secure.

FERGUS: What the fuck—

Dil speaks unnaturally quietly.

DIL: So tell me what you're doing, Jimmy.

INTERIOR. HOTEL ROOM—MORNING.

Jude, fully dressed. She takes a gun from under the bed and slips it in her handbag.

INTERIOR. DIL'S FLAT—MORNING.

Dil crouching beside Fergus, his gun in her hand.

DIL: Didn't really listen last night. I heard but I didn't listen.

Fergus, staring at her. He tries to pull on the bindings.

DIL: That won't do you no good. Dil knows how to tie a body.

She stands up, still pointing the gun at Fergus.

DIL: Wondered why you came on to me like that when you gave me the look.

FERGUS: He asked me to see were you all right.

EXTERIOR. STREET—DAY.

Jude on the street. Maguire's car pulls up rapidly and she gets inside.

INTERIOR. DIL'S FLAT.

DIL: See, I fix on anyone that's nice to me. Just the littlest bit nice and I'm yours.

FERGUS: Stop it, Dil—

DIL: Just don't kick Dil and she'll be touched. Be nice to her and she'll be yours forever.

She looks at him, tears in her eyes.

DIL: See, I should blow you away, Jimmy. But I can't do that. Yet.

FERGUS: Let me go, Dil.

He drags at his bindings.

DIL: Why?

FERGUS: Got to be somewhere.

DIL: Try and go, then.

EXTERIOR. STREET BY BROTHEL—DAY.

The figure of the judge in the window. Outline of a woman. Jude and Maguire are in the car, parked across the street. They look toward a paper seller.

MAGUIRE: Where the fuck is he? Christ—

INTERIOR. *DIL'S FLAT.*

Fergus pulls furiously at his bindings.

FERGUS: Let me go for fuck's sake, Dil—or they'll be here—

DIL: Let them come then.

IN THE CAR. OUTSIDE BROTHEL.

JUDE: Can't stay here, Peter—drive around once more—

He drives off.

INTERIOR. DIL'S FLAT.

Fergus collapsed back on the bed, exhausted.

DIL: Just want your company for a little while longer . . .

EXTERIOR. STREET BY BROTHEL—DAY.

Maguire's car driving round once more. No sign of Fergus.

MAGUIRE: That fucker's dead—

JUDE: No, we are.

INTERIOR. DIL'S FLAT.

Fergus strains and roars from the bed.

FERGUS: You don't know what you're doing, Dil—

DIL: Never did . . .

MAGUIRE'S POINT OF VIEW—*the brothel door opening. The elderly judge comes out. The car with his security men guns up.*

MAGUIRE: Give me the shooter, Jude—

JUDE: You're crazy—

MAGUIRE: Give me the fucking shooter!

He grabs it from her pocket. Throws open the door and runs across the street. Jude dives into the driver's seat.

INTERIOR. DIL'S FLAT.

Fergus, pulling at his bindings.

EXTERIOR. OUTSIDE THE BROTHEL.

The judge walking toward the open door of the car, held open by his goon. Maguire, running toward him, gun in hand. The goon sees him. Maguire shoots as he runs. Once, twice, three times, four. The judge falls. The goon, hit in the arm, pulls an Uzi and returns fire. Maguire hit, still shooting. Other goons tear from the car. Mayhem, screaming. Jude hits the pedal on her car and screeches off. Maguire, dead.

INTERIOR. DIL'S FLAT—DAY.

Dil, dressed in the soldier's cricket clothes. She looks like a sweet little boy. She places a cassette in the tape deck—"The Crying Game" song. She comes to the bed, and points the gun at Fergus's head.

DIL: You like me now, Jimmy?

FERGUS: I like you, Dil.

DIL: Give me a bit more, baby, a bit more.

FERGUS: More what?

DIL: More endearments.

FERGUS: I like you, Dil.

DIL: Love me.

FERGUS: Yes.

DIL: Tell me you love me.

FERGUS: Whatever you say, Dil.

DIL: Then say it.

FERGUS: Love you, Dil.

DIL: You do?

FERGUS: Yeah.

DIL: What would you do for me?

FERGUS: Anything.

She begins to cry and lays the gun gently on his chest.

DIL: Say it again.

FERGUS: I'd do anything for you, Dil.

She pulls on his bindings to release him.

EXTERIOR. STREET.

Two police cars, sirens wailing.

INTERIOR. DIL'S FLAT.

Dil's face, close to Fergus's, as the stockings that bound his hands are nearly undone.

DIL: And you'll never leave me?

FERGUS: Never.

DIL: I know you're lying, Jimmy, but it's nice to hear it.

His arm is free. He strokes her hair.

FERGUS: I'm sorry, Dil.

She shudders with weeping. The music of the song plays in the background.

Jude walking through the open door, arms extended, holding a gun.

JUDE: You stupid shit— Once was bad enough. But twice.

Dil rises from the bed and points her gun at Jude.

DIL: You didn't knock, honey—

Dil fires, hits Jude. Jude falls and is writhing on the floor.

FERGUS: Dil!

JUDE: Get that thing off me, Fergus—

Dil walks closer, holding the gun and pointing it at Jude.

DIL: What was that she called you, Jimmy?

FERGUS: Fergus.

DIL: What's Fergus?

FERGUS: It's my name, Dil.

DIL: What happened to Jimmy?

JUDE: I said get it off me, Fergus—

Jude, on the floor, reaches for her gun. Manages to grab it.

DIL: What's she going to do, Jimmy? She going to blow you away?

Dil shoots again, like a child, playing with a toy. She hits Jude in her gun shoulder. Jude spins one way, the gun the other.

DIL: Was she there too? When you got my Jody?

Fergus screams:

FERGUS: Dil!!!

DIL: I asked you a question, honey—were you there too—

JUDE: You sick bitch—

As she raises the gun, Dil shoots her repeatedly, saying:

DIL: You was there, wasn't you? You used those tits and that ass
to get him, didn't you?

*Fergus screams from the bed. He rips free his other arm. Dil
shoots Jude in the throat, and she falls dead, covered in blood.
Dil turns the gun on Fergus.*

DIL: She was there, wasn't she?

FERGUS: She was—

DIL: And she used her tits and that cute little ass to get him,
didn't she?

FERGUS: Yes.

DIL: Tell me what she wore.

FERGUS: Can't remember . . .

*Dil points the gun at him, squeezing on the trigger. Then she
stops.*

DIL: Can't do it, Jimmy. He won't let me.

She looks at the picture; walks over and sits down in front of it.

DIL: You won't let me, Jody—

*She raises the gun and places it in her mouth. Fergus takes it
gently from her mouth and places it on the table. He lifts her up
by the shoulders.*

FERGUS: You've got to go now, Dil.

DIL: Do I?

FERGUS: Yes. Now.

DIL: Am I in trouble, Jimmy?

FERGUS: Not if you go.

DIL: Will I see you again?

FERGUS: You will, Dil.

DIL: Promise?

FERGUS: I promise.

DIL: Where am I to go, Jimmy?

FERGUS: The Metro.

DIL: Meet Col.

FERGUS: Yes. Say hello to Col.

He leads her out the door. Fergus goes back into the room, past Jude's body. Looks out the window to where he can see Dil, staggering down the street, through the crowds that have gathered. The wail of police sirens coming closer. He watches Dil run off, with her funny walk. Then looks down and sees the cop cars pushing through the knot of people around the house. He picks up the gun, wipes it with a rag to remove Dil's fingerprints. He turns to the picture of the soldier; talks to it.

FERGUS: You should have stayed at home.

He sits in the chair by the window, waiting.

FADE TO BLACK.

INTERIOR. PRISON VISITING ROOM—DAY.

FADE UP to reveal a large interior, with light streaming in the windows. Large barred doors open and a group of women come through, with parcels, children in tow, etc. Among them is Dil, looking resplendent. She walks past the rows of convicts with their families, up to a glass cage, where Fergus sits, waiting.

DIL: Got you the multivitamins and the iron tablets, hon—

FERGUS: Don't call me that—

DIL: Sorry, love. Now, the white ones are magnesium supplement—

FERGUS: Stop it, Dil—

DIL: I've got to keep you healthy, Jimmy. I'm counting the days. Two thousand three hundred and thirty-four left.

FERGUS: Thirty-five.

DIL: I'm sorry, darling. I keep forgetting the leap year. What am I supposed to call you then, Jimmy?

FERGUS: Fergus.

DIL: Fergus. Fergus my love, light of my life—

FERGUS: Please, Dil.

DIL: Can't help it. You're doing time for me. No greater love, as the man says. Wish you'd tell me why.

FERGUS: As the man said, it's in my nature.

DIL: What's that supposed to mean?

She shakes her head.

FERGUS: Well, there was this scorpion, you see. And he wants to go across the river. But he can't swim. So he goes to this frog, who can swim, and he says to him, "Excuse me, Mr. Froggy . . ."

CAMERA PULLS BACK, *and as Fergus tells the story of the scorpion and the frog, the music comes up*—"Stand By Your Man."

THE END

VINTAGE INTERNATIONAL

The Ark Sakura by Kobo Abe	$8.95	0-679-72161-4
The Woman in the Dunes by Kobo Abe	$11.00	0-679-73378-7
Chromos by Felipe Alfau	$11.00	0-679-73443-0
Locos: A Comedy of Gestures by Felipe Alfau	$8.95	0-679-72846-5
Dead Babies by Martin Amis	$10.00	0-679-73449-X
Einstein's Monsters by Martin Amis	$8.95	0-679-72996-8
London Fields by Martin Amis	$13.00	0-679-73034-6
The Rachel Papers by Martin Amis	$10.00	0-679-73458-9
Success by Martin Amis	$10.00	0-679-73448-1
Time's Arrow by Martin Amis	$10.00	0-679-73572-0
For Every Sin by Aharon Appelfeld	$9.95	0-679-72758-2
One Day of Life by Manlio Argueta	$10.00	0-679-73243-8
Collected Poems by W.H. Auden	$22.50	0-679-73197-0
The Dyer's Hand by W.H. Auden	$15.00	0-679-72484-2
Forewords and Afterwords by W. H. Auden	$15.00	0-679-72485-0
Selected Poems by W.H. Auden	$11.00	0-679-72483-4
Another Country by James Baldwin	$12.00	0-679-74471-1
The Fire Next Time by James Baldwin	$8.00	0-679-74472-X
Nobody Knows My Name by James Baldwin	$10.00	0-679-74473-8
Before She Met Me by Julian Barnes	$10.00	0-679-73609-3
Flaubert's Parrot by Julian Barnes	$10.00	0-679-73136-9
A History of the World in 10½ Chapters by Julian Barnes	$11.00	0-679-73137-7
Metroland by Julian Barnes		
Talking It Over by Julian Barnes	$10.00	0-679-73608-5
The Tattered Cloak and Other Novels by Nina Berberova	$11.00	0-679-73687-5
About Looking by John Berger	$11.00	0-679-73366-3
And Our Faces, My Heart, Brief as Photos by John Berger	$10.00	0-679-73655-7
G. by John Berger	$9.00	0-679-73656-5
Keeping a Rendezvous by John Berger	$11.00	0-679-73654-9
Lilac and Flag by John Berger	$12.00	0-679-73714-6
Once in Europa by John Berger	$11.00	0-679-73719-7
Pig Earth by John Berger	$11.00	0-679-73716-2
Gathering Evidence by Thomas Bernhard	$11.00	0-679-73715-4
The Loser by Thomas Bernhard	$14.00	0-679-73809-6
A Man for All Seasons by Robert Bolt	$10.00	0-679-74179-8
The Sheltering Sky by Paul Bowles	$8.00	0-679-72822-8
An Act of Terror by André Brink	$11.00	0-679-72979-8
The Game by A. S. Byatt	$14.00	0-679-74429-0
Passions of the Mind by A.S. Byatt	$10.00	0-679-74256-5
Possession by A. S. Byatt	$12.00	0-679-73678-6
Sugar and Other Stories by A. S. Byatt	$12.00	0-679-73590-9
The Virgin in the Garden by A. S. Byatt	$10.00	0-679-74227-1
Exile and the Kingdom by Albert Camus	$12.00	0-679-73829-0
The Fall by Albert Camus	$10.00	0-679-73385-X
The Myth of Sisyphus and Other Essays by Albert Camus	$9.00	0-679-72022-7
The Plague by Albert Camus	$9.00	0-679-73373-6
The Rebel by Albert Camus	$10.00	0-679-72021-9
	$11.00	0-679-73384-1

VINTAGE INTERNATIONAL

VINTAGE INTERNATIONAL

VINTAGE INTERNATIONAL

VINTAGE INTERNATIONAL